DARK COCKPIT

DARK COCKPIT

How to Communicate, Lead, and Be in Control at All Times Like an Airline Captain

Capt. EMIL DOBROVOLSCHI

OCTAVIAN PANTIȘ

Fresno, CA

Published in the United States by
Ignite Press
5070 N 6th St. #189
Fresno, CA 93710
www.IgnitePress.us

ISBN: 978-1-953655-64-6 (Amazon Print)
ISBN: 978-1-953655-65-3 (IngramSpark) PAPERBACK
ISBN: 978-1-953655-66-0 (IngramSpark) HARDCOVER
ISBN: 978-1-953655-67-7 (E-book)

For bulk purchase and for booking, contact:

Octavian Pantiş
office@qualians.com

Library of Congress Control Number: 2021903032

Original text in Romanian
Translation to English by Dina Climatiano
Original cover design by Alexe Popescu for Publica
Edited by Pat Iyer and Reid Maruyama
Interior design by Alexe Popescu for Publica and Eswari Kamireddy

To Mădălina and my children Irina, Ioran, and Matilda. You provide thrust to my every flight.

—E.D.

To my wife and our three children. Sometimes we're in a dark cockpit, sometimes we are not, but the journey with you is beautiful every day.

—O.P.

Contents

Preface | How and Why Was This Book Written

I met Captain Dobrovolschi in 2008 while flying on vacation with my family. The flight itself was uneventful, but what caught our attention was the pleasant manner in which the captain addressed the passengers from the cockpit – clear and concise, but also friendly. Often when you hear the captains' announcements, it sounds like they're holding their nose and that they're mostly in a hurry to finish the chore. This time, every passenger on the plane knew precisely what the route and conditions would be like and what they would see on the left or the right at any moment. It made us feel like genuinely welcome guests on the plane.

Over the years, Emil and I got to know each other better, and I had the privilege of hearing many stories from his vast experience as an airline captain and a flight instructor. It dawned on me that quite a few of those stories hold valuable insights that could be useful to anyone:

- How to communicate effectively
- How to lead responsibly
- How to be in control at all times

This control is essential especially in stressful situations. While any cardiologist would advise against confronting problems that test your very limit, someone who has done his homework will be able to handle them calmly.

Together we have presented these stories and insights at many live and virtual conferences to dozens and sometimes hundreds of people. Every single time, the feedback is incredible, and people are glued to their seats. Through the links we make between the world of aviation and day-to-day life, we inspire our audience to think about their cockpit. Not only are they up for the challenge, but they always want to know more, and, as a conclusion to every session, they seek to understand the rules and procedures of aviation better so they can apply them in their own lives, be it at work or home.

I suggested to Emil that we write this book to be of use to anyone who wants to improve themselves, which is undoubtedly a lot more people than we could ever meet at a conference. I wanted us to write it so people can go back at any moment and consult the helpful advice found in this book, apply it in their daily lives, fully experience it, and also be able to share it with their colleagues and kids.

Emil immediately agreed, so we got to work. Emil provided critical pieces of information about the world of aviation, along with a long series of carefully selected examples and events. My role was to identify the insights that would be most useful to you, organize the information in a way that is most suitable for a "how-to" book – like the one in front of you – and to fit it all in a clear, easy-to-follow format. The fruits of our labor await you in the following chapters.

Because this is a book authored by two people – we each had a hand in every chapter – we had to ask ourselves how we could avoid clumsy wording. For the sake of simplicity, and since the experiences described in the book are Emil's, we thought it appropriate that the narrative voice should be his.

Statistically speaking, air travel is by far the safest way to get from place to place. The aviation industry holds itself to the highest standards and uses the most efficient procedures to ensure safety. Within the pages of this book, you'll find ideas, examples, advice, and questions born of these same standards and practices designed to boost your confidence and guarantee the best results for your journey.

Good luck!
Octavian Pantiş & Emil Dobrovolschi

Introduction | What Is a "Dark Cockpit"?

"Good morning, ladies and gentlemen, and welcome on board!"

I must have said this sentence thousands of times. You must have heard it plenty of times yourself. Now it takes on a whole new meaning because I am inviting you on a unique journey – into the cockpit, the world of aviation, but also your world. The principles and ideas within the pages of this book can help you improve your life tremendously.

Now, as you step onto the plane, instead of dawdling down the aisle past the other passengers to your assigned seat, come with me into the cockpit, that mysterious place, softly lit by multiple screens and hundreds of little light bulbs, about which you've probably always wondered. Perhaps you caught a glimpse of the pilots through the half-open door, sitting with their headphones on, getting ready for takeoff. Maybe on other occasions, the cockpit door swung open upon landing because the plane hit the ground just a little too hard, allowing you a peek at the pilots in action as they stopped the plane on the runway. It happened to me a couple of times before our doors were modified to be more secure. I could always feel dozens of curious eyes stabbing me in the back of the neck.

Join Me in the Cockpit

Come, explore the cockpit, and find out what a "dark cockpit" is and why that is the most fitting title for this book.

The first thing you notice about the cockpit/flight deck is that it seems too tight a space for the multitude of devices, buttons, screens, and switches of all shapes and sizes crammed into it for no apparent reason.

There are so many controls that, at first glance, it seems impossible for anyone ever to understand and remember what every gadget does. The sheer amount of information is overwhelming, and your brain simply refuses to absorb so many details all at once.

The first thing you notice about the cockpit/flight deck is that it seems too tight a space for the multitude of devices, buttons, screens, and switches of all shapes and sizes crammed into it for no apparent reason.

Don't worry. This is perfectly normal. Everyone has that reaction when first setting foot in a modern cockpit. I usually let my guests take it all in and relax a bit before I tell them anything about this interface between the pilots and the aircraft – the cockpit.

The Screens

Let's begin. In front of you, on the front panel, there are several screens. These show all the information that has to do with the functioning of the plane's systems and engines, temperature, and pressure gauges. These screens are also where we find vital information about the plane's speed, altitude, position, and trajectory. There are two sets of screens in the cockpit – one for each pilot. In the center, we find the autopilot controls. On the horizontal panel between the captain and the copilot are the navigation computers and the control levers for the engines and the flaps.

When you break it down into bits, the cockpit isn't nearly as scary anymore, is it?

The Buttons

Above your head is a panel with hundreds of buttons of every color and form. The buttons are responsible for the operation and control of the plane and alert the pilot to malfunctions. Here we also find the controls for the fuel, hydraulics, pressurization, air-conditioning, engine fire extinguishers, electrical systems, and others. These all connect to hundreds of computers, pumps, valves, relays, and switches positioned along and across the plane. Each one of these has knobs, dials, and buttons on the overhead panel in the cockpit.

When you break it down into bits, the cockpit isn't nearly as scary anymore, is it?

Flight decks have always been complicated. For many years, their complexity required many more people in the cockpit to handle and operate the many buttons and levers while also flying the plane. When I first started as a pilot in 1994, a standard flight crew consisted of five people: two pilots, a flight engineer, whose job was to supervise and operate the plane's systems, a navigator, who handled the plane's trajectory and air navigation, and a radio operator, who was responsible for radio communications. Accommodating five people meant the cockpit was much larger than it is now. Nowadays there are only two people in the cockpit.

The Pilots

I intentionally left out the two large armchairs covered in unique white synthetic fur, probably the first thing you see when you enter a cockpit. In a typical aircrew, the pilot in command (PIC) occupies the left chair. The copilot sits in the right. This setup has an ergonomic design that allows each pilot to see all the indicators in the cockpit and operate all of the plane's systems from the seat and also reach the control column, known as a *yoke* in Boeing airplanes and a *sidestick* in Airbus, which maneuvers the plane.

No matter how modern and automated an aircraft might be, without the two pilots, it would just be a metal pipe filled with seats, miles of electrical cables, engines, actuators, pumps, and switches, all just lying around for nothing. The pilots' will and actions make flight possible. Both have earned their positions through a lot of hard work: courses, ground school, flight simulations, and flight training – all of which took many years to complete.

But pilots never really finish their training.

They get regular tests to maintain a high proficiency level and make sure they are always prepared to handle emergencies. Both training and testing occur in Full Flight Simulators (FFS), capable of recreating any flight scenario in conditions that are identical to a real cockpit (for more details, see the index at the end of the book).

In some training flights, the plane doesn't land on the optimal touchdown zone on the runway. Less experienced pilots argue that "the plane pulled" to the left or the right as if it were a giant being, whimsical and complex, who usually listens to us but who sometimes has a will of its own and does whatever it wants. Pilots get a lot of training for landing in crosswind situations. They are trained to know where they touch down, how they land, and

But pilots never really finish their training.

whether they should choose to abort landing and go around. The emphasis is on teaching them to be in control, and not be passive.

Meet My Overcoat

Whether I'm flying an ATR 42 or 72, Airbus 318 or Airbus 310, with 48, 120, or 275 passengers, I always think of the plane as a sort of overcoat that I put on when I enter the flight deck. I wear it from takeoff until landing, safely and comfortably, doing things the way I want and the way they should be done, regardless of the weather outside or any problems that may arise on the way.

I always say that the plane's length or width makes no difference; the pilot still flies it from the cockpit.

The controls are the same, and all the buttons are in their usual place.

You might not be a pilot, but your life is your plane. It is your overcoat, and you decide what to do with it every day. Maybe you've recently taken on responsibility for a project. That is your plane, and your job is to get it from where it is to where it should be; all the while, you're in the cockpit, holding the controls.

I always say that the plane's length or width makes no difference; the pilot still flies it from the cockpit.

Color-coded Lights

Now that you're familiar with the flight deck, let me introduce you to the color codes – an essential part of successfully managing the complex cockpit.

A white light indicates system elements that have not been

powered. The word OFF is lit in white to show that specific pumps, generators, valves, or other components are not active.

A blue light indicates a system or an element that the pilots have intentionally turned on, that has not been activated automatically. The word ON is illuminated in blue to indicate that one of the plane systems is using something deliberately, causing additional consumption of resources. For example, this occurs when one is using the de-icing system, which removes ice from the plane while airborne.

An amber (yellow) light indicates a minor malfunction that does not require the pilots' prompt intervention. Amber means CAUTION, and an audible alarm, a single "bing" sound, accompanies it. In the overhead panel, a malfunction in one or more of the systems is marked by FAULT in amber. While a single amber light does not necessitate urgent attention, several concurrent amber lights – meaning multiple minor defects – may imply an entirely different and potentially serious scenario.

Red means WARNING, and it is also accompanied by an audible, repetitive alarm that does not stop until the pilot executes specific actions.

A red light is associated with a major malfunction, defect, or an especially critical situation that requires the pilot's immediate intervention because it compromises the flight's safety.

Red means WARNING, and it is also accompanied by an audible, repetitive alarm that does not stop until the pilot executes specific actions.

As a passenger, you may hear a pilot announce in a soothing tone that a light came on while the plane was waiting for takeoff. It invariably means returning to the gate so the engineers can determine the significance of the light. This is an essential maneuver to assure the safety of the passengers.

Dark Cockpit Defined

What is a dark cockpit? That is what we call a situation where no lights are on – no blue for extra usage, amber for caution, or red for danger. Everything is going smoothly. Everything is under control and working within its normal parameters. The plane is flying, and the passengers are doing their own thing: reading a book, watching a movie, having a snack, fiddling with an Excel spreadsheet, making friends, or simply taking a nap.

That is how we want all flights to be – in a dark cockpit. That is also why engineers designed the cockpit the way it is so that the lights do not distract us from flying the plane.

To achieve this state of a dark cockpit, pilots need to put in a lot of work and check many things. They must use the plane's systems correctly and make sure they do not exceed any operating limits.

In the context of this book, a "dark cockpit" is a lifestyle in which you strive to keep things under control, anticipate and predict possible problems, minimize stress, and handle things with ease and efficiency.

Non-dark Cockpits

Sometimes there are situations in life where it is impossible to maintain a dark cockpit, like the birth of your first child. In such moments, your life is more likely a Christmas cockpit, not a dark one, because it is full of little lights in all colors that keep going on and off.

Some people might have a CAUTION light on when the baby is asleep for too long (meaning two hours), and they're worried their child might go hungry, the poor thing. Should I wake him up and give him something to eat? No, let him sleep. And when the baby coughs a little, that is an immediate WARNING. The same cough might turn on a mother-in-law's WARNING light because she opened the window in the next room just as daddy walked by with the baby snuggled up in a towel after a bath. In this situation, life becomes one twinkle after the other.

At work, how dark is your cockpit? For some, it's Christmas every day.

But let me ask you this: when was the last time you had a dark cockpit? Indeed, there were periods, some shorter, some longer, way back when or maybe even recently, when it all went smoothly. What was the context? What were you doing so well? Can you recreate the experience?

At work, how dark is your cockpit? For some, it's Christmas every day.

Amber and red lights are not the only ones that cause stress. Blue lights can be just as distracting because they represent additional effort, a sprint that is not sustainable.

In the next chapters, you will discover how we pilots plan every mission, how we communicate efficiently, how we interact with our crew, and how we deal with times of crisis.

There are many similarities between my job and other professional fields. I am sure that in your field, you also encounter challenging situations that force you to think on your feet and make split-second decisions, just like a pilot. In the next chapters, I challenge you to think about the concepts illustrated in the real-life examples and apply them to your life.

I want you to learn how to do what you want and what is needed,

In this book, you will discover how to harness each member of your team's potential and significantly increase your chances of success using a few simple communication and assertiveness rules.

and at the same time, have everything under control. That is what we all set out for every day, isn't it? I also want to show you that the success of any endeavor, or a flight, if you will, is never the result of dumb luck or the work of an individual; it depends not only on our hard-earned experience and skills but on our attitude as well.

In this book, you will discover how to harness each member of your team's potential and significantly increase your chances of success using a few simple communication and assertiveness rules.

I encourage you to use this book to find out how you can "dark cockpit" your way through life, be it at work or home.

Part One | Communicate Unequivocally

1 | 100 Knots! Check

Now that you are familiar with the cockpit, it's time you tried your hand at flying – first in a simulator, then, eventually, on a plane.

Critical Communication Skills

A pilot must enunciate clearly and use the appropriate tone and rhythm when communicating a message to the copilot or air traffic control.

The first thing that you notice about pilots is the way they communicate with each other. In the flight deck's semidarkness, we sometimes don't see each other very well with our eyes forward. We always wear headphones, in which we hear overlapping and slightly distorted radio transmissions. (At first, I couldn't even understand what people said in my native language, let alone English!) The environment is generally loud due to the fuselage's friction with the air and the engines' noise. Despite these distractions, pilots receive training to execute procedures word-for-word and communicate unequivocally.

A pilot must enunciate clearly and use the appropriate tone and rhythm when communicating a message to the copilot or air traffic control.

The timing of the announcement is also crucial. The message needs to be quite precise – for example, when executing a specific action or when informing of a deviation from standard parameters, the pilot must announce any changes in parameters or work procedures. After checking the flight instruments for the announced changes or actions, the other pilot confirms the communication loud and clear. The confirmation serves as an affirmation that the pilot understands the message, has taken action, and they are ready to proceed to whatever they need to do next.

Why is communication so important? Why do we do everything in our power to convey messages quickly and clearly? In aviation, the stakes are exceedingly high. With hundreds of people on board, we want to get everyone to their destination safely and as comfortably as possible, *every time.*

Also, there are up to 25,000 planes in the air at any given moment – that's a whole lot of planes! On some routes, they can get pretty close to one another. Such heavy traffic wouldn't be sustainable without effective communication between each airplane and air traffic controllers and between the planes themselves. Take, for instance, the aircraft congestion around major airports, where takeoffs and landings take place every minute, and there are always 10 to 15 planes waiting to take off or land. This intricate air traffic system, which has become an essential part of our world, would simply not be possible without excellent communication.

You, too, can get familiar with this professional way of communicating and discover how we exchange messages. At times, some of the content might surprise you, and you might wonder whether some of these communication loops are actually necessary. The important thing is to extract a few rules of thumb, principles by which you can improve your communication with your colleagues, your team, and even your family. It will make your life easier, relieve you of unnecessary and avoidable stress and misunderstandings, and help you reach your goals more easily.

Check!

The title of this chapter – *100 Knots! Check* – must seem a bit odd at first glance. Let's see why we chose it for this particular part of the book.

Picture this:

- We're in the cockpit
- Boarding is complete
- We finished the preflight checklist
- We're at the beginning of the runway
- We're about to set the throttles and take off

The takeoff airspeed is typically around 155 mph or 250 km/hour – the exact number is calculated in advance, accounting for different factors. But before we get there, we need to work our way up to that speed. To you, as a passenger, that mostly means you feel how you're pulled back into your chair a bit as we move faster and faster.

When the plane reaches a speed of 100 knots, meaning 115 miles per hour, the pilot who is monitoring announces "100 knots," and the pilot who is flying needs to confirm the "Check." If the other pilot does not promptly answer "Check!" the takeoff is aborted. *Immediately.* The same happens if the pilot not flying does not make the initial "100 knots!" announcement when the plane reaches the respective speed.

How does that sound? A bit weird, isn't it? By this point, the pilots have spent about 45 minutes of intense communication together in the cockpit. If one of them had had a problem, the other would have noticed by now. They have just gone over all the systems, making sure everything is in order. They got the OK for the takeoff. Everything is set, but now the flight has to be stopped, with all the consequences of lost time and costs, and panic bound to ensue, only because one of the pilots didn't say "Check!" quickly enough.

Yes, that stoppage is precisely what the procedure demands.

Yes, that stoppage is precisely what the procedure demands.

To understand the role of such messages in assuring any flight's success and safety and the importance of communication in general, I invite you to walk a mile in a pilot's shoes and venture on the same path they do in their training. Let's start with the FFS – the Full Flight Simulator.

The Full Flight Simulator

A crucial step in the training of any professional pilot is the simulator. In addition to their initial training, pilots must attend a minimum of two four-hour sessions every six months, culminating in examinations in conditions identical to reality. They are tested on their knowledge, skills, airmanship, and, most importantly, their ability to apply all of those in a given situation. What happens if the pilot fails even one of those four annual exams for any reason? The airline suspends the pilot from flying and sends the pilot to remedial training, first in ground school, then back in the simulator.

This technological marvel, the FFS, can accurately recreate the cockpit and everything that might happen during a flight, from everyday situations like takeoff and landing to emergency scenarios.

The simulator allows pilots to see, hear, and feel everything as if they were on a real airborne plane.

Imagine the front part of a plane replicated in a simulator. The cockpit is perched on six cylindrical piston arms that move rapidly and independently of each other to reproduce the roll, pitch, and yaw of the aircraft and the accelerations, decelerations, and the trepidations experienced in flight. The concave screens project the terrain around an airport, including highways, buildings, roads, and houses at an angle of view of 175°, resulting in quite an impressive 3D image.

What's Real and What's Fake?

The simulation can take place in any airport in the world. Like Innsbruck, Bolzano, or Funchal on the island of Madeira, some destinations explicitly require that the pilots flying there are trained for them specifically. The simulation is so detailed that if you're already familiar with the chosen airport, you can peep into the neighbor's pool, or watch tourists dining at the seaside restaurants, or simply admire the picturesque fishing villages along the coast.

The simulator can also authentically render the stunning contours of some of the world's most impressive mountain ranges, so if you happen to be a trekking enthusiast, you might recognize some of the valleys, gorges, and peaks. The instructor can set the simulation to any time of day, including gorgeous sunrises or sunsets, in any weather conditions – from clear skies to a raging blizzard with rain, thunder and lightning, snow, or strong winds. The simulator shows all of these meteorological phenomena. It also mimics their effects on a real airborne plane, so the pilots are wholly immersed in the experience within minutes.

Emergency!

Pilots also receive training to handle improbable situations, ones that have never happened in real life, as well as ones that simulate recent incidents or accidents.

Depending on the specifics of the session and the subjects selected for the training or exam, the instructor gradually switches from the typical stages of flight to critical situations: losing an engine on takeoff, a fire in the engine following a bird strike, smoke in the cabin, hydraulic or electrical malfunctions in the control systems, depressurization of the passenger cabin, or any other scenario for which the pilots need to prepare.

Pilots also receive training to handle improbable situations, ones that have never happened in real life, as well as ones that simulate recent incidents or accidents.

In a three-year cycle, pilots should be instructed and examined on all the exceptional cases described in the operating manual. I mention this to serve the book's direct objectives and reassure you that you are in good hands when you get on a plane.

My First FFS

To this day, I remember my first FFS session – I was in Toulouse, France, training for a copiloting position on an ATR 42 aircraft. The instructor, an Italian senior with mounds of experience, spent ages looking at the new programs that had just been uploaded onto the latest simulator system, along with some special "upset recovery" exercises. These exercises included having the pilots close their eyes while the instructor puts the "plane" in unusual positions. The simulator could be, for instance, nose up vertically, or in a 90-degree incline, nose pointing down, a positioning that could happen in storm clouds or severe turbulence. Subsequently, the instructor asked the pilots to open their eyes exactly when the instructor "handed over the plane" to them in that unusual position.

We include exercises such as these in the pilots' training because in the unlikely event a passenger plane manages to get into that position we need to know the correct maneuvers to right the plane. The two pilots must know exactly what to do, even though the required maneuvers are neither intuitive nor easy to execute. In addition to operating the control column and the rudders – the primary controls of any plane – the pilots also have to handle the engine throttles swiftly. At the same time, the aircraft accelerates and decelerates dramatically, depending on its position.

This FFS was the instructor's first time laying eyes on the new simulator program. He accidentally activated one of the scenarios, and we found ourselves hurtling down in a perfectly vertical plane. The simulator made a leap to mimic the acceleration, so the instructor was thrown into his seat and couldn't reach the FLIGHT FREEZE button in time.

Meanwhile, we were screaming our heads off, desperately trying to take control of the aircraft, which was headed straight towards an exquisitely contoured green plain filled with clusters of trees. We were too low to reverse the position, but we both pulled the control column with everything we had. I later discovered that simulators have a safeguard called "*crash inhibit*" that doesn't allow maneuvers that are too sudden, but we didn't know that at the time. For us, the dive was so real that we needed a coffee break to get our knees to stop shaking so we could get on with the training session.

The Value of Briefings

Today, after eighteen years of experience as a flight instructor (it makes me wonder how old the Italian from ATR was), I start every simulator session by briefing my students. (I describe the briefing below.) The training manual outlines the briefing's length and synopsis. Still, regardless of how many sessions I've led in the previous week or month, I like to add a personal touch to this part of the exam because I know how necessary tests are to any pilot.

I prepare for each day of examination as if it were my first. Every pilot is different, and the way each might understand or interpret a training standard can vary from one pilot to the next. There are clear guidelines for how to evaluate and analyze a pilot's performance that instructors must respect. In the past, older instructors told me about an additional standard that doesn't appear in the manual. This is the additional standard:

If you, the instructor, trust the pilot to fly your own family, your children, based on their performance in the examination, then you can let them pass with a clear conscience.

If you, the instructor, trust the pilot to fly your own family, your children, based on their performance in the examination, then you can let them pass with a clear conscience.

Before starting the session, I always try to explain in my briefing the context and the theory behind a particular regulation or a standard, why we communicate in one way or another in certain situations. And here we get to the most interesting part for you.

The Rebels: No Room in the Plane

By the time they approach the simulator, all pilots are already familiar with the standard procedures, but some try to rebel and refuse to follow them strictly. Sometimes it's because they don't fully understand them; sometimes it's a matter of convenience. Beginners, or worse, the undisciplined, usually have the greatest resistance to an SOP (Standard Operating Procedure). Sooner or later, they all fall in line because they will not be permitted to fly otherwise.

Think about traffic laws and the test you need to pass to get your driver's license. Most people know the laws, and yet every time we drive, we come across drivers who break the most basic traffic rules (like not crossing a continuous white line) without giving it a second thought.

While irritatingly common for drivers, in aviation, there is zero-tolerance for rule-breaking.

Not only are SOPs described in great detail, but we follow them religiously to the letter; *there is no room for negotiation*. The way I see it, following an SOP should come as naturally as breathing or the beating of the heart.

Over the years, I have enjoyed flying with other SOP-abiding pilots worldwide: New Zealand, South Africa, the UK, Austria, Germany, Italy, China, Portugal, and France. No matter where my copilot was from or what accent each of us had when speaking English, when we exchanged looks after another successful landing, we knew beyond any shadow of a doubt that we all spoke the same language in the cockpit.

While irritatingly common for drivers, in aviation, there is zero-tolerance for rule-breaking.

Standard Calls

Every SOP begins with a standard call, a particular communication reserved for a specific situation. The execution of the SOP comes only after that. There are standard calls – specific expressions – for many conditions and contexts. One of them is *100 knots! Check*. We'll get back to that in a bit. Another – *Glide slope! Correcting* – you may have noticed is the title of Chapter 3.

Keep in mind that it is impossible to have a standardized message for every conceivable predicament. If you find yourself in an unprecedented situation, it is on you to find the quickest and most effective way to make sure that others understand your message.

Pilot Roles

During the flight, one of the pilots is the Pilot Flying (PF), responsible for the maneuvering of the aircraft, the trajectory, and the speed. The other is the Pilot Non-Flying (PNF) or Pilot Monitoring (PM), who is in charge of radio communications, keeping track of and operating the plane's different systems, and monitoring the PF. Usually, the flight commander (PIC) is the one to decide who does what at any given moment.

You Have Control

I was flying an Airbus 310 from New York to Bucharest. We were somewhere over Germany, at FL 390, another flight crew's standard forms of communication, fast and efficient. It is an acronym for "flight level three nine zero." It represents the altitude in hundreds of feet – in this case, 39,000 feet, which is almost 12,000 meters.

We were both happy that we would soon go home after a relatively long haul with terrible turbulence over the Atlantic Ocean. I was the Pilot Monitoring, and just as I was on the radio confirming the German air control's message, the autopilot suddenly went off, its alarm came on, the plane started to *ascend* lightly, and my copilot shouted, "You have control!"

As I mentioned earlier, the *commander* is usually the one to hand over or assume control of the aircraft. The standard communication for that is, "You have controls, I have communications," followed by a swift confirmation, "I have controls," at which point the copilot takes on the role of Pilot Flying. In a reverse situation, the commander says, "I have controls," and the first officer confirms, "You have controls," so I was caught slightly off guard by my copilot. I should have been the person to state I would assume control.

Of course, while I was talking to the air traffic controllers, they heard the autopilot's decoupling alarm and saw that we were climbing past the agreed-upon altitude. They thought we were having difficulties and asked for clarification, ready to aid us. I quickly told my colleague, "You have controls," pushed the control column a bit to maintain our altitude and got on the radio again to assure the Germans that everything was under control.

The above describes a typical convergence of seemingly trivial events coinciding with poor communication in the form of an incomplete standardized message.

I was already annoyed with the copilot, who couldn't even keep the plane horizontal without the autopilot, not to mention that *he* gave *me* an order! Then, for the second time in the three or four seconds since the autopilot had gone off, I heard, "You have control!" That was the final straw. I looked at the copilot to understand if he was somehow incapacitated, and I saw that all of his flight instruments were blacked out – he was flying blind. This temporary malfunction affected only his side of the flight deck and resolved itself within minutes.

The above describes a typical convergence of seemingly trivial events coinciding with poor communication in the form of an incomplete standardized message.

The copilot did the only thing that made sense to him, considering he had no guidance – he told me to take control of the plane. But I didn't understand him because, at that exact moment, I was on the radio, and my flight instruments did not indicate a malfunction. We were both in the same cockpit, but we were flying two different planes in a way. He could have avoided this misunderstanding had he briefly described the problem before saying, "You have control." These exchanges are exactly what we watch out for in a simulator session and discuss in detail with all the training participants.

This is why communication is vital. Pilots must keep track of each other's actions in the cockpit to make sure they are "on the same page," in sync with each other on what stage of the flight they're in or the procedure they're executing. There are rare, unusual, and challenging cases when the pilots must act independently of each other, as if the cockpit were divided in two, until they begin the landing, when both pilots are required to focus on the same elements.

The Sterile Cockpit

It is so essential for the pilots to respect communication discipline that there are specific thresholds or limitations for certain communication types. For example, under FL 100 (about 3,050 meters), the flight deck is in a state of *sterile cockpit*. The pilots are not allowed to do anything but operate the plane. The only conversations that are permitted must exclusively relate to the operation of the aircraft. This rule was introduced in 1981, after research had established that *non-essential* conversations between crew members were among the leading causes for several accidents because they distracted the crew from the landing procedures or prevented them from retaining vital information, like the plane's actual distance from the ground.

And now we finally get to dive into *100 knots! Check*. We are in a *sterile* cockpit. As takeoff is a critical moment in the flight that includes a few standard calls and thresholds, we must execute them quickly because whether the plane takes off or not depends on the response. If it is anything but quick and decisive – meaning, if there was no response, or even if there were slight indecisions like a short pause – the plane would stop on the runway. The purpose of this is to ensure the overall safety of the take-off and landing.

There is no idle chat, no small talk, no useless commentary, no hesitation, and no incomplete responses because the margin of error is practically nonexistent.

There is no idle chat, no small talk, no useless commentary, no hesitation, and no incomplete responses because the margin of error is practically nonexistent.

In those moments of terrifying acceleration, when those 100,000 or 200,000-horsepower engines pull the plane up to the required rotation speed, communication has to be punctual and precise. When the plane reaches 100 knots, accelerating towards the end of the runway, you have to ascertain that both pilots are conscious and have not been compromised in any way after the rapid acceleration, be it for personal reasons or because they got hit by something in the cockpit. *100 knots!* Therefore, "check" is a crucial bit of communication, used in a critical moment in the flight to ensure that everything is OK and that we can safely lift off.

Use Standard Language

By making sure that they are indeed "on the same page," the pilots can help each other with their tasks or take full control of the plane, no matter how critical the situation gets. Using standardized language eliminates many misunderstandings and language barriers.

The emphasis put on this discipline and standardization in communication ensures the unequivocal transmission of messages between the two pilots in the cockpit, with air traffic control, and the cabin crew.

In difficult cases, when there's a fire and passengers need to evacuate, there must be clear communication between the pilots and the firefighters.

What is your takeaway from this? What can you apply in your day-to-day life? For example, what is your equivalent of a sterile cockpit? Have you ever found yourself driving your car under tricky conditions, and asking your passenger to not talk until you got through the crisis? You've probably figured out other examples of situations. Maybe you even took some notes or underlined key ideas on this page if you're holding a printed version of the book.

The emphasis put on this discipline and standardization in communication ensures the unequivocal transmission of messages between the two pilots in the cockpit, with air traffic control, and the cabin crew.

Critical Communication Patterns

Here are three communication habits that would make things go a lot more smoothly:

1. Communicate Even When It Doesn't Seem Necessary

This statement might remind you of the joke about a conversation between a married couple:

"Dear, you haven't told me you loved me lately, and I'm worried that you don't love me anymore."

"Sweetheart, I told you I loved you 20 years ago when we got married. If anything changes, I'll let you know."

Now, this is hardly the picture you had in mind for that first bit of advice, is it? You were probably thinking more along these lines: Maybe you haven't heard from your teammates in days about the project you're coordinating. You're tempted to believe that everything is going well. Perhaps it is, or maybe things got stuck, and no one is saying anything because the situation is "not critical" yet. But time wasted now may cost you dearly later.

The truth is most people choose not to communicate because they make assumptions.

The truth is most people choose not to communicate because they make assumptions.

Some assume something positive, like "Everything is going to be OK." Others tend to have a more negative inner dialogue: "I shouldn't bother them now, I can already see them raising their eyebrows at me" or "I don't think they'd go for my idea, I better keep it to myself." But none of this gets the job done any faster or better, so stop assuming and start asking questions. Talk to your people, find out what's going on, and shine a light on what's important.

Think of a situation when you communicated something – via email or phone, in a meeting, or in any other way. You assumed the matter was closed and that you had done an excellent job, only to discover later that people's reactions were completely different from your expectations.

We all know that a message needs repetition many times and, in many ways, to truly get through to people. That is what advertisers do through the medium of commercials, what parents and teachers do with kids. It's also what lovers do to avoid having conversations like the one above.

There is a popular expression in change management: "You can't over-communicate." It means that no matter how often you communicate, it is never too much.

Think about your relationship with your clients, subordinates, or other people you work with daily – what are the critical moments that could benefit from a "*100 knots! Check*"? What are the vulnerable stages of a project or a process, where you can't afford to make assumptions, and it is better to ask again than to stay in the dark?

Pilots probably say, "100 knots!" and "Check!" dozens, hundreds, even thousands of times, and it probably feels like a complete waste of time because everything is always OK – until the one time it isn't. The other hundreds of exchanges suddenly seem vital at that one time, when a pilot is incapacitated for whatever reason, and the other pilot realizes it on time and prevents a disaster.

2. Start with the Facts

"We have to reschedule the meeting" is a message that is bound to be met with a prompt "why?" because it is an incomplete communication. Correct or not, it is your subjective conclusion, provoked by either an external cause ("The client isn't coming") or an internal cause ("I'm not satisfied with how my presentation turned out"). Either way, rescheduling the meeting may indeed be the right decision, but there could also be better alternatives.

Most of the time, it is better to start with the facts. Describe the situation as it is, as neutrally as you can – no interpretations, no generalizations, without automatically leading the discussion to a position that is favorable to you. People catch on, sooner or later.

If you put all the facts on the table, then you can decide together, or leave it up to the boss, the client, or whoever else. If you start with the facts, you can save yourself unnecessary stress and even embarrassment. If you try to manipulate the situation, it might come crashing down on you.

Manipulation is the killer of relationships.

Let's say that you have a meeting with someone. You show up on time, but they are not there. You have a choice here. You can fall prey to negative thoughts from mild to severe: "That one's always late. What can you do? Some people can't get their head out of the clouds" or "They don't respect me and the value of my time" or "They're making fun of me."

You have a choice as to how you handle your reaction. Suppose you give in to your resentment. They finally show up; you greet them with some snide remarks. Your simmering anger taints your chance of accomplishing much.

Manipulation is the killer of relationships.

Or you could stay calm, and when they show up, you say, "It's 11:30, and you scheduled the meeting for 11:00. I would have appreciated a message if you knew you wouldn't make it in time."

If you manage a calm, "It's 11:30" and then, after a short pause, "We said we'd meet at 11:00," you won't even need to say anything else because they would unquestionably come in with some insincere apologies by now. Let the facts do the talking for you. Imagine how you would feel if you resentfully berated them, only to find out they just came back from the hospital ER after watching their father being admitted for chest pain.

When you combine "Communicate even when it doesn't seem necessary" with "Start with the facts," you could message or call the person the morning of your meeting. Ask, "Are we still meeting today at 11:00?" You will save yourself emotional energy that you could better spend elsewhere.

Start with the facts. Show that you're in control of the situation, show that you've prepared, that you are not bothered by inappropriate feelings.

As a bonus, you'll maintain and strengthen the relationship.

3. Standardize as Much as Possible

Every communication loop is closed with a confirmation like "Check!" or a repetition of the message, such as "my controls/your controls." What are the areas in your life that have open loops?

For example, on Tuesday, a client asks you to finish something by Friday. You decide that you'll handle it on Thursday but overlook responding to the client's request. The client doesn't know that you will do it on Thursday and that everything will be OK. Maybe the client thinks you haven't received the message or have received it but that you can't deliver and that you're taking your time to figure out how to respond. A short reply like "OK, you'll have the report by Friday" would set everyone's mind at ease.

As a bonus, you'll maintain and strengthen the relationship.

What can you standardize? When the rules are clear, your daily activity becomes a lot less stressful, and the unavoidable mishaps become much easier to handle.

The late Peter Drucker used to say, "Don't make 100 decisions when one will do," meaning we all have situations that we deal with frequently. We can decide what to do and how to communicate every time one of them occurs, or we can make a single decision about how we do things, establish a procedure, a set of messages that we need to communicate in a given situation. The "If This, Then That" app is useful for automating some of those activities. Developing strategies takes a bit of time, but you can be sure they work once you do. Just like SOPs in aviation, you can update your procedures from time to time, but together they form a valuable asset to any company.

What can you standardize? When the rules are clear, your daily activity becomes a lot less stressful, and the unavoidable mishaps become much easier to handle.

The safety of the flight is the most crucial consideration in modern aviation. All communications serve this purpose. You, too, have important considerations, standards you're trying to keep, and goals you want to achieve. Make sure you support them and help them flourish through the way you communicate. *100 knots! Check.*

2 Unique in My Uniform

My job makes me a bit of a weird passenger to have on board. You might see a blue-and-white plane, but I see an Airbus 320neo, with LEAP motors and sharklets (vertical extensions at the end of an Airbus wing).

Pilot on Board

When we enter the plane, we both greet the flight attendants, but I also check out their uniforms and compare them to ours. You look for your seat; I look to see how far my seat is from the emergency exit. If you do that, too – good for you!

While we're still at the gate, the other passengers flip through magazines, fiddle with their phones, or look out the window at the hustle and bustle around the plane; but I keep an eye on how long it takes to refuel, how much more baggage needs to go into the cargo hold, and which ground handling company is handling the plane.

I check my watch to see that we're not losing our slot. Before I even set foot on the plane, I already know what the weather is like at take-off and landing and throughout the route, and I know how long the flight will be. Most of the time, I also mentally evaluate the captain for how they welcome the passengers on board over the PA.

When I was an instructor at ATR, an aircraft manufacturer founded in France, I would often travel to Toulouse, which was, at the time, home to the only European training center with ATR 42/72 flight simulators. For years I flew there regularly, sometimes even twice a week, so I knew by heart all the airports we would pass on the way. I'd fly from Paris with one of our sister companies, which used the same type of planes we did. Sometimes, I even recognized some of the cabin crew – all good professionals: a little distant, but welcoming, like true ambassadors of their company.

The Maverick Pilot - Is He Any Good?

Coincidentally, I also happened to fly several times with the same captain, who was quite the maverick, like a movie character. The first time I saw him, I was shocked. I stopped dead in my tracks at the plane entrance, forcing the passengers behind me to bump into me. I was convinced I was on one of those hidden camera TV shows and that there were concealed cameras around us, just waiting to capture our reaction to this prank.

The sight of him took me aback: Imagine a guy in his fifties, with golden-blond locks down to his shoulders but also a generously receding hairline, partly covered by a baseball cap that read CAPTAIN in gold embroidery. Three or four of his shirt buttons were undone, enough to reveal a gold cross dangling from a massive chain on his hairy chest! He flashed a charming smile and casually invited the passengers on board his plane. What would you do? Wouldn't it give you pause? Wouldn't you expect the captain of an aircraft to be a little more dignified or professional?

He seemed like a decent fellow, even if he was a bit "ostentatious," but just to set your mind at ease after that jarring first encounter – he was a professional through and through. After all, he was a pilot in one of the largest and safest airlines in Europe. Still, what was it about him that made us all hesitate to board the plane? How would you react if you've never flown before, and just as you're about to take your first steps inside an aircraft, you come across this character, presented to you as the captain? If you recall in Chapter 1, I explained that there is no room for rebels inside the plane.

First Impressions Count

Many psychological studies have demonstrated that people form their first impression of a person within mere seconds of laying eyes on them for the first time. Ninety percent of the people we meet form their opinions of us in the first few seconds! This first impression tends to turn into cement and becomes immutable. In other words, it is tough to convince people that their perception of you is wrong after they have already made up their minds. Pretty sad, huh? Annoying, even. We professionals who have worked so hard to master our craft – whatever it may be – are so much more than the dictionary definition of our vocations: pilot, doctor, engineer, marketer, manager, or whatever else. Of course, we're free to choose how we dress, style our hair, or wear a baseball cap.

I'm convinced that every one of us is so much more than our appearance suggests. Still, the question remains – why was I reluctant to get on a plane flown by this maverick of a captain? Well, wouldn't you hesitate to let a surgeon with tattooed arms operate on you? In this situation, some people would be tempted to ask for a different doctor because something about this image doesn't quite add up. People have definite preconceptions of how a professional in any field should look. If the professional's appearance deviates from that – that's it! They pass a verdict; they already have an opinion; they have labeled the professional, and labels are hard to remove.

Let me clarify – I don't have anything against tattoos or individual styles of clothing. I'm only confirming what you already know yourself, which may not be fair, but it happens every day: It doesn't take long to make a first impression, and often, whatever happens next is more likely to reinforce that first impression than change it. That's all. Maybe one day things will be different. Some people may be better at resisting their initial instincts and postponing their judgments until they are better acquainted, but reality usually proves otherwise.

I'm sure I've given into that initial instinct myself. If our flamboyant Frenchman had "slammed" the plane on landing, I might have blurted out: "That's right, slam it right into the ground. Maybe if you buttoned up and shaved, the landing would go smoother." Whether I would have said it or not is irrelevant. Truth be told: Pilots with immaculate uniforms and a James Bond hairdo can also sometimes slam the plane a bit on landing, and perhaps in their cases, we might only say: "Come on, it went well, considering the weather."

When you meet someone, even before you utter a single word, your appearance speaks volumes.

Knowing all that, how important is it for us to make a positive first impression? How important is it for you?

When you meet someone, even before you utter a single word, your appearance speaks volumes.

A professional's reputation is their competence in their area of expertise, as well as the way they look and dress. I can guarantee that no one would get on a plane with the best pilot in the world if that pilot sported a mohawk dyed green and orange if they could instead fly with someone who fits the image of a captain.

Your appearance is the window to your attitude. One of the most important things about a captain – or anyone – is attitude. It is so important that we have dedicated a substantial chunk of this chapter to it. People often ask me how to determine someone's attitude. The first indication is always their appearance, their posture, and the way they look. What does *your* appearance say about *you*?

The Value of a Uniform

Things are a little simpler for us aviators. We wear uniforms. Have you ever wondered why all pilots in all airlines always wear uniforms? After all, air traffic controllers don't wear uniforms. Architects – extremely well-educated people who constitute an essential trade in our society – don't wear uniforms. Engineers don't wear uniforms.

There are many reasons we wear uniforms in commercial aviation, but we primarily do so because uniforms help ensure and communicate the standard that we set for ourselves. We want to project a professional image that breeds trust and reassures the passengers of our competence from the first contact.

It doesn't matter if you're a man or a woman, tall or short, thin or chubby – the uniform commands respect. It is a state of mind.

The neutral colors, the classic lines, and the universal ranks – four stripes for commander, three stripes for copilot or first officer, two stripes for copilot in training (second officer), and one stripe for chief purser – are all elements designed to convey calming authority. People tend to feel safer flying with a crew who wears uniforms as opposed to a crew who shows up in a mismatch of jeans, sweatpants, and Hawaiian shirts.

In addition to identifying us, uniforms are also practical. Passengers can quickly identify who to listen to and who to follow in case of an emergency.

For example, let's discuss a nerve-racking situation in which uniforms prove priceless: an emergency evacuation taken under less than favorable conditions. Maybe it's dark; maybe there's smoke; perhaps the aircraft is at an odd position because it veered off the runway and one of the landing gears broke; maybe a fire erupted in one of the engines, and it's burning through a wing full of fuel, impossible to put out with onboard fire extinguishers.

Uniforms and authoritative non-verbal communication (the subjects of this chapter) and strong, standardized messages (which we discussed in the previous chapter) make the difference between an evacuation where no one gets hurt and one that ends in the hospital. It is the difference between getting to go home at the end of the day (albeit late and stressed) and far worse outcomes.

The Evacuation Steps Made Easy

Let me walk you through an emergency evacuation. It doesn't start immediately after the aircraft stops. As a passenger, stay calm and keep in mind that it will take a little while and that the delay is for your safety.

First, suppose the plane landed and caught fire. An *emergency procedure* is initiated to stop the engines and notify the control tower about the emergency – *Mayday, Mayday, Mayday.* Do you know what the commander's next course of action is according to the procedure? *Nothing.* Not one of the tasks on that list is the commander's. The commander only turns his or her chair back to get the best possible overview of the copilot's actions, inform the control tower, and assess all available information to make a good decision. The goal is to determine where the fire and smoke are going to spread and how to get the passengers off the plane as quickly and safely as possible.

- Which direction is the wind coming from?

- At which intersection between the runway and the taxiway has the plane stopped?
- What dangerous substances are in the luggage hold?
- How much fuel is in the wing?

If necessary, the captain turns on the PA (Public Addressing) and tells the passengers to evacuate the plane, then notifies the tower, and orders the copilot to leave the aircraft.

The last to evacuate the plane is the captain, who leaves through the back exits to ensure no more people are on board. Their duty doesn't end there – there could be panicked passengers running straight towards the fire trucks coming towards the aircraft at full speed. That is another moment when the uniform proves crucial.

One's attitude shows in one's demeanor.

My 28-year-old colleague, the youngest captain in our company, is 1.6 meters tall (5'2") and weighs 50 kg (110 pounds). When she wears her captain's hat, sharp uniform, and has appropriate verbal messages at the ready, I can guarantee that all eyes are on her.

You may be thinking, "OK, I now understand the importance of a uniform in aviation, but surely you're not suggesting we all start wearing uniforms from now on, are you?" You're right; I'm *not* telling you to stock up on uniforms starting tomorrow.

One's attitude shows in one's demeanor.

Attitude Equals Demeanor

Whether we have an impeccable uniform on or not, the way we choose to present ourselves in society makes us look a certain way. People will also judge our attitude in no small part based on our appearance. Attitude is often the "golden standard." We may prefer to work with someone who has a good disposition even if their competence is lacking. Similarly, a bad attitude might be a deal-breaker even if the candidate is exceptionally well-versed.

Appearance Equals Competence

Just to illustrate my point, I'll give you an example: About two-thirds of candidates interviewing for a pilot position never go into the simulator to demonstrate their flying aptitude. They never even get to show how good they truly are because *they don't make it past the HR interview.* Why is that?

A copilot I once trained for his first Type Rating (a simulator exam) is an excellent pilot today and an instructor to boot. He has over ten years of experience flying for foreign companies, and he has made quite a name for himself: He's been selected as a TRI (Type Rating Instructor) and TRE (Type Rating Examiner). He was an Airbus 320 commander when he *failed* his first interview at a huge, well-known Asian airline. I couldn't believe that he didn't pass the interview. I knew him very well, and we are close friends, so I asked him what had happened. He didn't know what went wrong.

At the end of the interview, they only thanked him for his time and told him that he was a quite experienced pilot and captain, but he simply didn't fit the company profile. We went over the interview together, analyzed the questions they had asked him, how he handled the trick questions, and it seemed that he conducted himself precisely as he should have.

I couldn't figure out where he fell short until he described what he wore to the interview. He was around thirty years old at the time, and he was very self-conscious about how he dressed, always trying to be trendy. Because the interview took place late in the evening in a London training center, he went for a bold smart-casual look: jeans, a light-colored shirt with the top three buttons undone, and a pistachio-colored blazer.

What can we learn from this story? Maybe the interviewers were relatively superficial – they judged the book solely by its cover.

> Even if you don't wear a uniform, you should still be mindful of what you wear.

Perhaps that particular airline missed out on an excellent pilot, but in those conditions, with twenty pilots vying for the same position, they also took note of the candidate's attire.

Conforming to a dress code doesn't mean you have to put on an act. You might be the kind of person who wears jeans and sandals, but if you want to look professional, you have to adapt yourself to your surroundings at least a little bit.

It goes both ways, too – it is possible to be overdressed: how would you look if you went to a barbecue in a suit and tie?

Even if you don't wear a uniform, you should still be mindful of what you wear.

Ask yourself what your outfit says about you. Workplace dress codes have relaxed quite a bit in recent years, which is not a bad thing – there were too many penguins hanging around office buildings. But there is a balance. Nowadays, some people show up for work looking like they've just come from a pajama party. The point is that whether you like it or not, your appearance says a lot about you.

Uniform as a State of Mind

Consider a uniform as a metaphor for how you present yourself to others, from colleagues to business partners. If you want efficient communication, aside from how and what you say, you have to wear the right "uniform."

- When you're with your kid, you should wear your "dedicated parent" uniform
- When you present a new project at work, wear your "competent colleague" uniform
- When you speak in public, do it confidently and show that you're leader material

Indeed, after years of experience, you have all those uniforms in your metaphorical dresser. To guarantee optimal communication, all you have to do is match your uniform to the message you want to convey.

But how do you make yourself stand out when you wear a uniform? I have been wearing the same uniform for the past twenty-six years, and as it is inherently a uniform, we pilots all look the same when we wear it. Pretty dull, isn't it? But every person has a unique personality, and even if the job involves a lot of procedures and restrictions, there are plenty of opportunities to display your uniqueness. I decided to "accessorize" my uniform to make it easier for me to reach my goals and communicate better.

Accessorize Your Appearance

The handiest accessory is my smile. I have a positive outlook on things, and I've long since discovered that no matter how big or difficult an obstacle is, it is much easier to overcome if I throw a little optimism into the mix. How could athletes walk onto an arena if they didn't tell themselves they're the best and that they will succeed no matter how hard it gets? And it's not just you who benefits from it.

The confidence you exude when you're master to the situation is contagious.

Showing it dramatically improves your entire team's chances of achieving success.

"You May Encounter Some Turbulence"

I've often had to take off through storm clouds, and I knew that up there, we would have to use the onboard radar to avoid areas with medium to severe turbulence. Other times, I took off towards home knowing that we had some minor malfunctions – a few CAUTION amber lights, which the operation manual may permit. Still, the captain must always make the final decision to take such a risk.

> The confidence you exude when you're master to the situation is contagious.

In a problematic flight, I explain to the crew what we have to do and address the passengers and tell them what's going to happen and how we're going to proceed. My communication always ends with them thanking me after we've landed, as they're disembarking, regardless of how bumpy the flight.

Another accessory that adorns my metaphorical lapel is emotional control. I will tell you more about this one in Chapter 7. For now, I want you to know that it is possible and that you can even use your emotions to your advantage so that you are always in control. It is yet another way to be unique in your uniform, especially when you find yourself in high-stakes situations where you have to bring your "A" game.

Your Attitude Counts

Attitude assessment is always masked as something else.

I often prepare foreign copilots for job interviews at different airlines in various countries. Before we'd meet, you would find out the sort of questions these companies typically ask in an interview, their requirements for pilot and copilot positions, and what they expect to see in a candidate. We would work on all of those questions together.

We would dedicate the better part of our time to the attitude you should demonstrate at the meeting, precisely the focus of this chapter. I'm not teaching you how to lie or pretend to be someone you're not. Not only is it *not* something I would do myself, but it wouldn't be of much use anyway – interviewers are trained in identifying such things.

> Attitude assessment is always masked as something else.

So, what's the secret? What do interviewers want? We're going to go into a little more detail in the next few paragraphs, and the reason we're going to do that is simple.

You can't fix something you don't recognize.

Maybe you went to your fair share of interviews in the past and got rejected, but you never learned why. You might have thought the reason was one thing, but in reality, it was something else entirely. Maybe it wasn't an interview but a sales pitch – you tried to present an idea to your boss, or a project to your board, or you offered a service to a client – but you couldn't close the deal and had no idea why. Perhaps you even asked and got an answer, but it might not have been the real reason. As long as you are not clear on why you fail – or succeed, for that matter – you run the risk of bombing yet another interview, pitch, or meeting.

When you interview for a copilot position, you're likely to get questions that appear to test your proficiency in theory, SOPs, and technical problem solving (and if you can't answer any of those, you might as well not show up at all). But your interviewers, with their seemingly never-ending knowledge questions, are trying to shake you up, to get you to "break character." They're trying to see beyond the façade you've put on for the interview, and they do it by making you lose your cool and forcing you outside the comfort zone of having all the answers.

Let me give you an example of such a question: "If we hired you, and on one of your flights, your commander misconducted themselves or gave you orders that explicitly defy the SOP – for instance, to go below the minimum altitude for landing – and you were the Pilot Flying – what would you do?"

What would your answer be?

Just Culture

In aviation, we have what is called a *non-punishment environment* (also known as *just culture*). Suppose someone makes mistakes during the flight (like exceeding certain limits, however slightly, or breaking SOPs), and they are reported immediately after landing. In that case, there will be no negative consequences for the flight crew.

There will be questions, the scope of which is to determine what went amiss in communicating the procedures and their execution. Still, the questioner will ask them neutrally, not in the form of accusations. After all, pilots are human, and knowledge gaps regarding different planes or other flight safety elements are not unknown. In the end, depending on the findings, the pilot will receive recommendations for ground or simulator training.

We don't have punishments or fines because we wouldn't want pilots to be afraid to get into the cockpit the next day and make a mistake. That fear will only add to their stress level, which is not conducive to good decision making. When training paradigms were less forgiving in the old days, you'd be more afraid of making a small mistake in front of the pilot-in-command than of a flaming engine.

Today, we prefer pilots make decisions that are right for their respective flight and concentrate on that and nothing else because our main concern is to get the plane and the passengers to their destination safely. We don't want them to get distracted by thoughts like, "What will the flight director say when he sees I've added a maneuver there?" Still, if there is any intentional violation or lack of discipline, the offending pilot will not be allowed to continue flying, and it's almost certain that they will be fired and lose their license.

What Would You Do?

Getting back to the question above: "What would you do if your PIC gave you an order that blatantly violates procedure?" Everybody knows the standard answer. You say, "My controls" and take over the aircraft. If it were only a test of knowledge, the interviewer would have ticked it off as correct and moved on. But instead of moving on, they bombard you with questions to try and see right through you. As soon as you calmly (or maybe with slight irritation) say, "I announce, 'my control' and take over the plane," they ask you if you're sure.

Maybe it is a critical situation, and they continue to ask you a variety of follow-up questions:

- Are you just going to take over from the commander, ignoring their experience in similar situations?
- Are you ready to take on the responsibility of those stressful

moments, those crucial seconds in the span of which you have to make a decision?

- Will you do that when you know perfectly well that everything in the cockpit is recorded and eventually analyzed when there's a possibility you'd be held responsible for many deaths?
- And how exactly are you going to proceed?
- What if you misunderstood the commander?
- Wouldn't you ask them to repeat the message?
- Would you just go ahead and take control of the aircraft?
- You're not as experienced as the commander – what if you make the wrong split-second decision?

The manual doesn't describe all scenarios. And you know that in some cases, if following the SOP may endanger the flight, maybe there is room for deviation. Maybe that's what the commander is doing – deliberately breaking the SOP to secure the flight. Are you really just going to say, "My controls"? What if the commander refuses? Would you wrestle the controls out of their hands?

What's at Stake?

Imagine this kind of exchange – even as a mere spectator, or, if you feel like getting your heart rate up, picture yourself in the candidate's chair. The conversation has long since left the realm of friendly chit-chat. They have already gone over your track record, and now, maybe an hour after the initial pleasantries, the future of your career is at stake. Sure, you may already have a gig as a copilot, but perhaps you came here for a bump in the salary, or to relocate with your family to a better country, or to move up the ranks and become a commander yourself. Even if it weren't about more money or improving your quality of life, no one likes to botch a job interview. One thing is for sure: you wouldn't be here if you weren't serious.

Your interviewers are also serious.

Dead serious. They know that if they hire you, they're trusting you with a $100 million plane and their multi-billion-dollar company's decades-long reputation. And with something a lot more valuable – the lives of over 200 passengers who count on you to get them to their destination.

Your potential employers need to know that you're the real deal. If you were in their place, wouldn't you do everything in your power to be sure? Wouldn't you try, repeatedly, from different angles, to test the candidate's resilience, way of thinking, personality, and attitude? Without a doubt! You would spend hours meticulously planning the perfect ordeal that would target and expose all your candidate's weak spots.

Your interviewers are also serious.

But you're in the interviewee's chair. Three people with much more experience than you scrutinize your every word, every movement, every pause, and every look. It is about so much more than your knowledge – it's about your *attitude.* If they only wanted to test your knowledge, they would be satisfied with an online test or have an intern mark your answers on a form – but no. They want to stress you out, catch you off-guard to see how you'd react. For them, the easiest thing you could do is fail because then they simply don't hire you. No harm, no foul. That is why some of them want you to fail because then they get to go home relaxed. They're practically itching to find any fault that would let them off the hook.

It's when you don't strike out, when you give all the right answers and show the right attitude – that's when they realize they might have to sign off on you, and then the whole world will know, even ten years later, that they're the ones who gave you their seal of approval. In a way, *their job depends on your performance*, so you can be confident that they will test you time and again, going over your flaws, however small, with a fine-tooth comb. Do you understand now why those guys from the Asian airline wouldn't take a chance on my friend in the jeans and pistachio-colored blazer?

If your car driver skidded a bit and hit the fencing, you can simply step out of the car, but on a plane, it's a bit more complicated. That is why the process of hiring pilots is so rigorous.

What's the Answer?

Perhaps you're wondering what the answer to the question above should be. First, you need to control your emotions, just as you would when flying. Failure to do so will hurt your credibility and keep you from thinking straight and giving the right answer. As for the answer, we need to consider the context: You're interviewing for an airline whose standards for selecting pilots are quite high. If the interview for a copilot position is so grueling, imagine how uncompromising the process of becoming a commander must be.

In any airline, pilots who achieve commander status do not exhibit a lack of discipline like the one your interviewers described without a good reason, or they simply wouldn't be given that responsibility. Of course, it is still possible for such a capable person to make a mistake or give the wrong order, but in that case, the best course of action is to respond with a standard call or turn their attention to the problem at hand and help them get back on track. If, after that, you still think that the commander is putting anyone's life in danger, then – and only then – will you jump in and take control of the plane.

Maybe you've never had an interview like that, by the end of which you are entirely beat and a pound or two lighter. If we stop and think about it, though, we have all had encounters that we now think of as turning points. What made the difference?

It was likely your attitude rather than your knowledge.

After all, attitude is the "uniform" with which you present yourself to others, not only in a meeting with a client or at a job interview, but daily, with every person you meet. The components that make up your appearance – your smile, your hair, your clothes and accessories, your rhythm, your posture – these are all things that can reinforce or completely undermine what you say.

It was likely your attitude rather than your knowledge.

How do you communicate unequivocally? By not giving people reasons to doubt you.

To conclude this chapter, let's outline two essential points.

1. When it comes to clothes and accessories, they need to look good and fit the context and surroundings. It is not about the brand or the price but about the way you wear them.
2. Everything about you that people can see is an introduction; it's just a part of a whole that defines you. I mention this now because it is essential – your appearance can block or facilitate communication, but it does not replace hard work and professionalism, which should still be at the base of success.

I've met exceptional commanders who couldn't care less about how they looked but performed remarkably throughout their careers. I have also met many *copilots* who spent their entire career, right up until retirement,

How do you communicate unequivocally? By not giving people reasons to doubt you.

looking like they came out of a catalogue but couldn't or simply didn't want to become commanders.

The bottom line is: Be yourself. Establish an attitude that is right for you – one that doesn't tire you but helps you do whatever you have to do and whatever you want to achieve every day.

3 | Glide Slope! Correcting

I was scheduled to fly to Istanbul one afternoon. Imagine my surprise when I found out who my copilot was going to be: a very green and very, very young pilot, a new hire at our company. When I say young, I mean I almost asked to see his ID to make sure he was over 18! A blond-haired, blue-eyed, red-faced bundle of nerves: he knew that he was about to fly with an instructor-examiner, who was also a test pilot. (I'll tell you later about the type of maneuvers we pull with a plane when we first get it from the manufacturer). I also was his superior because at that time, I was the Director of Flight Operations at our airline. A three-in-one!

I tried to show him that there was nothing to be afraid of – I don't bite. We did a thorough pre-flight checkup, I explained how to prepare the cockpit step by step, and I told him that I would fly the first leg towards Istanbul.

It was a flight like any other flight, nothing out of the ordinary. The weather was perfect – *Calm Cavok 1013,* as pilots say – and it was *dark cockpit* all the way there. Still, something did happen after we began preparations for landing at Atatürk Airport. To land on Runway 5, you have to make the final approach over the water, which means descending over all sorts of vessels, big and small. We had disengaged the autopilot and guided the plane towards the runway "by hand."

In the short final, I saw a jet-ski in the water doing the most unbelievable acrobatics. It was distracting enough to make me take my eyes off the flight instruments for a second and deviate half a point from the optimal landing slope. It wasn't too bad – half a point is not much of a deviation, almost unnoticeable. Still, that was the moment – my young copilot's time to shine. I heard him say, "glide slope!" and though I didn't think it possible, his baby face turned an even deeper shade of crimson.

Let's *freeze* for a minute and analyze this scene, what he could have done and how I could have reacted, and what you could do in similar situations, whether you're the PIC or the copilot. The plane is hovering in place, as is the jet-ski and the other aircraft – everything is frozen. I'm going to give you some context, break it down, and then we'll go back and see what happened.

The Right Command at the Right Moment

Glide slope! is a standard call – a concept we have already defined in Chapter 1: a specific message that has to be communicated at the right moment. This particular message is how the Pilot Monitoring informs the Pilot Flying of a deviation from the correct path of descent.

I could have handled this in several ways. The one outlined in the manual is to say "correcting," which means you got the message, and you're immediately adjusting your course to re-enter the glide path.

But at that moment, both the copilot and I had a decision to make, a choice of three different approaches for how we could handle the situation.

3 Reactions to Glide Slope!

You have these same three approaches at your disposal when things don't go your way. Of the three, only one is a healthy response; avoid the others.

In aviation, we could take this statement a step further and go for an unequivocal distinction: Only one approach is correct, and the others are just plain wrong.

You have these same three approaches at your disposal when things don't go your way. Of the three, only one is a healthy response; avoid the others.

But what are those three approaches? They're nothing new; we all know them from childhood. We have seen different people take them, or we've used them ourselves. They have been here long before we ever came along, and they will be here long after we're gone.

1. **The Submissive Approach:** When something is wrong, as the observer, you can always hold your tongue or merely suggest an answer. This approach has many names: from "passive," "defensive," and "submissive" to the more colloquial "shy" or "sheepish." When you go for this approach, you don't change a thing, either because you value the relationship too much, you don't care about the outcome, or some mix of these and other reasons. Pilots have crashed planes because someone was too afraid to speak up.
2. **The Aggressive Approach:** The second approach is where you say what you need to say, but how you say it, the tone you take, offends the other party. The message itself gets across, but due to a heightened state of stress, anger and hostility are also being communicated.
3. **The Assertive Approach:** In between those first two

approaches, another one exists – the assertive approach. This is when you say your piece, but you stick to the facts, and you don't attack the other person in any way. You assert yourself, but you also maintain an even, composed demeanor.

The Assertive Approach

All communication in aviation was designed with the assertive approach in mind. Take *100 Knots!* for example. The pilot does not make up what he or she wants to say. The procedure specifies the right response: the somewhat dry but efficient "check!" When the Pilot Flying deviates from the landing slope, the Pilot Monitoring doesn't go "Excuse me, perhaps you can check the screen as something seems to be less than perfect," but keeps it brief and to the point, avoiding room for any unnecessary passivity or aggression – "Glide slope!"

The Correct Response

What could I have said to my young copilot? Well, I could have ripped him a new one. I could have told him that it wasn't even half a point over the intended slope or that I did it on purpose, just to see how he'd react. I could have put him "in his place." After all, at that point, I had already clocked in 10,000 hours of flying – how many did he have that he allowed himself to tell me I was wrong? And why was he so red in the face, anyway?

Sure, it happens to the best of us: We decide to stand up for ourselves, we choose to be assertive, but we're not entirely confident, or maybe we're even a little afraid of how the other person might react, especially if it is someone that we consider superior in one way or another.

Anyway, I chose the standard response, "correcting," and immediately made the adjustments.

In that moment, I knew that I was sitting next to a future commander, a true professional who wouldn't let social barriers and customs stop him from following procedures, no matter how awkward.

As experienced commanders, we have the responsibility to "groom" our copilots. We encourage them to give us feedback. When we hear them say "check speed," it doesn't even cross our minds that they think we're unprepared or that they're insinuating anything but that the speed we are maintaining is ten knots above what the flight instruments should indicate. I know that I have a trustworthy professional who helps me stay the course, allowing me to focus on the bigger picture, taking in more details, and making better decisions.

In that moment, I knew that I was sitting next to a future commander, a true professional who wouldn't let social barriers and customs stop him from following procedures, no matter how awkward.

Deciphering What Went Wrong

After deciphering the black box in aviation accidents, investigators listen to the CVR (Cockpit Voice Recorder). Nowadays, these systems are so sophisticated that not only can you listen to the conversations in the flight deck, but you can make out any noise on the recording. You can even place the sounds, as there are several stereo channels from which you can figure out the sound's source.

Ultimately, the investigators match up this soundtrack with the record of the plane's journey, so you can hear what the pilots were saying while they were maneuvering the aircraft. Most of the time, the communication continues right up until the crash itself. It is vital to analyze how it transpired – the tone and the exact wording.

Sometimes you hear the commander barking orders or arguing with the copilot. Other times, when the commander makes serious errors in judgment, we regrettably find out that the copilot was *utterly silent*. In other words, in those crucial moments, the pilots communicate in one of the three ways we've mentioned: submissive, aggressive, or assertive.

We all use a mix of those three every single day. To better analyze their effects, imagine two combs, each one has three "teeth," and they're facing each other. Worded another way, imagine a capital E and its reflection in the mirror. These represent two people. The top "tooth" represents a submissive approach, the middle assertive, and the bottom aggressive.

Let's add one more detail to the image: a thin line that connects one E's "tooth" to the other's.

This line marks the approach used by each of the two people. For example, if the line passes through the two E's middle teeth, both individuals are assertive. See how balanced that image is? That is exactly what we want in the cockpit, at work, and in any other interaction.

We've left a little space here in the book. If you will, please grab a pen and draw the two E's facing each other, same size, with the middle teeth on the same horizontal line – please draw that too, from one side to the other. If you read this as an ebook, please grab not only a pen but also a piece of paper. Drawing the figure yourself will make the message so much more memorable to you.

Be sure to draw the two E's big enough so you can write "Submissive" on the top tooth of the E, "Assertive" on the middle one and "Aggressive" on the bottom one. Write the same words on the same lines on the other E. Now you have the complete picture.

When the horizontal line connects the middle teeth of the two Es (or combs), then we have "glide slope!" from the copilot's right E and a "correcting" from the commander's left E. From now on, whenever you see a capital E, think of those three approaches and try to be *assertive* in what you want to say, no matter how convenient it may seem to give into submissiveness or how tempting it may be to blow off some steam with the aggressive approach.

If you want to work your imagination a little more, push the left E up a bit so that the communication line starts at the bottom tooth towards the right E. Now push the right E down so that the communication line touches its upper tooth. If I managed to make myself clear, what we're looking at here is an aggressive-submissive combination. In the world of aviation, if this approach had a name, it would be "Korean Air," and it led to two decade's worth of disasters.

A Case Study: Korean Air

Between 1970 and 1999, Korean Air and its predecessors had a long and sad history of incidents and accidents, resulting in the loss of 16 planes and over 700 lives. In some of those cases, the weather was perfect for flying. There were no technical malfunctions found in most of them, as the planes in question were both new and modern – and yes, planes can be new, but not modern, as you'll see later in this chapter.

Overall, the pilots in question tested well above average in both knowledge and performance. Hijackings, onboard bombs, and getting shot down by fighter jets caused some of these accidents. However, the majority of the incidents, including ones that necessitated Soviet military intervention because of unscheduled breaches of Soviet airspace, were mainly due to miscommunication in the cockpit, specifically – the lethal combination of a submissive copilot and an overly-confident commander who, in moments of uncertainty, resorted to aggressiveness, at least from the point of view of the copilot.

Those incidents' investigations uncovered the "uniqueness" of Korean culture, with its long tradition of total respect towards one's superiors and rigid adherence to hierarchy. The way one addresses their elders or higher-ups is quite nuanced and restrained and cannot be initiated at any time. For example, a direct address may be downright rude in some situations.

For a copilot to notify the commander that the latter has made a mistake is considered impertinent, no matter how grave the error. Picture that culture in the cockpit; imagine having to act under those constraints in times of crisis or key moments for your team. All this to say that these traditions and institutions created a culture of miscommunication that led Korean Air to be considered one of the most dangerous airlines in the world. Luckily, the situation has changed now.

"Did We Forget to Do Something?"

The most important thing to remember about miscommunication is that one can avoid it.

So let's look at *one* of the dozens of incidents that critically damaged Korean Air's reputation to better understand what could be improved upon.

The plane is headed from Jeju to Daegu on June 13, 1991. You are the copilot. Out of the blue, and in a serious transgression from usual standards of operation, the commander decides that there's no need to do the *landing checklist*, which goes over everything needed to complete the procedure. The copilot says nothing. Consequently, the inevitable happens, and they forget to do something: They never lower the landing gear.

What's more, a few minutes after initiating the descent, the commander asks the copilot to deactivate the audio and visual alarm – the intermittent "bing" and the red WARNING light – which notifies the pilots that the landing gear is not down. Why did the captain want the alarm silenced? Well, according to the CVR, "It is irritating, and it is distracting me from the landing."

Finally, the commander lands the plane – a Boeing 727, with three engines in the back, two on the sides of the fuselage, and one above – on its belly, in an ear-splitting screech, sparks flying all over the place. All of the passengers scream their heads off, the commander is stupefied, and the entire airport is up on its feet. The landing destroys the plane, never to be used again. Thankfully, by some random stroke of luck, no one was hurt.

If you had been the copilot on that flight, what would you have said? What would you have done?

Sure, if you're one of those "short-fused" people I have the dubious pleasure of meeting sometimes, the outcome would have been much different, but you probably would have been put on trial for assaulting your commander.

Careful! It's easy to push your E up, bringing aggressiveness into the axis by giving free rein to harsh words. You can feel quite tempted because aggressiveness comes with the instant gratification of "unloading" your feelings. Maybe you know from your own or other people's experience that aggressiveness can be effective, setting the other person straight and making them do what you want. But we all know that aggression only breeds more aggression.

I can't tell you how many times I've seen both Es pushed all the way up, resulting in *mutually aggressive communication* – in meetings, in traffic, or even on TV, escalating a banal situation that people could have solved without either side having to lose anything. Instead, colleagues never recover their relationships, or even brothers won't speak to each other for years.

Don't take it as a personal attack if those around you notice your mistakes. Correct them and move on.

The correct solution – be it in the Daegu-bound cockpit, in my Istanbul-bound cockpit, in your team's meeting room, and at your family's dinner table – is assertiveness, regardless of what the other person chooses to do.

Don't take it as a personal attack if those around you notice your mistakes. Correct them and move on.

In the flight deck, you clearly need assertive-assertive communication. As exhibited in Korean Air, the aggressive-submissive combination is discouraged through the rigor with which communication standards are taught and upheld. In contrast, the combination of a submissive commander and an aggressive copilot is unfathomable. For one, on any flight, the commander has enormous responsibility, which wouldn't allow them to be passive. Additionally, no matter how relaxed the communication between two pilots is, copilots know their place, and there will always be some distance between them and the commander.

The Responsibility Falls Squarely on Your Shoulders

Can you be assertive in every interaction you have in your day-to-day life? Probably not. Plus, sometimes, if we let aggressiveness take over, we can regret what we say and do, not only *after* the fact but even *during* the act. We also know that a submissive approach may create distance in some relationships and cause tension to accumulate. Unfortunately, we may take this tension out on our loved ones, who are the least deserving of such treatment.

This chapter challenges you to apply assertiveness as often as you can. If you're always assertive, you will not only communicate better but also carve out a reputation for yourself as a person of principle, someone trustworthy.

Perhaps you're wondering: "Fine, but what do I do if every day I am bombarded with annoying problems that are clearly not my fault? And what do I do if I have to deal with all these problems with zero leeway? How can I stay assertive? When do I get to be angry and explode, just a little?"

Pilots face the same challenges. Although pilots are not the ones who caused the problem in many cases, the responsibility of solving it falls squarely on their shoulders because it is their mission to successfully land the plane with all its passengers safe and sound. Always. Maybe you too carry similar burdens, where you're the one responsible for the outcome regardless of the cause, only in your case, the problems occur on a weekly, if not daily, basis.

Aviation Safety

Let's look a bit more deeply at what causes safety issues. Considering the leading causes of accidents and incidents that have endangered passenger safety, let's divide the century-long aviation history into three distinct periods: technological failure, human failure, and airline failure.

It Is the Fault of the Plane

> The history of aviation is written in blood.

The first period is defined as one where technology was at fault for most accidents. In the first period, plane crashes were mainly attributed to the quality of engines and subassemblies and the industry's low level of quality. Planes were rudimentary. As aviation was a wholly new and unfamiliar domain, there were no standards for building plane components and spare parts or repairing planes. It was all uncharted territory, a novel field, revolutionary and fascinating, with bold and enthusiastic people.

The history of aviation is written in blood.

Still, the good aspect of the field's evolution – other than the joy and benefits of flying – is that the aeronautics industry learned a lot from its mistakes.

Over time, the world of aviation has seen tremendous progress. Modern airplanes encapsulate technologies so advanced that they go far beyond any device we use or come across in everyday life, from a technical point of view. Some of today's plane systems outperform the gadgets of our day, predating some by as many as two decades sometimes. Two decades! Look at the latest smartphone in the palm of your hand. Even if some of the devices used on the plane today look like the gizmos people currently use, the difference in quality is night and day.

I'll give you an example: In our aircraft, we have six LCD screens, each approximately 17 cm (6.6 inches), used to display all the information needed to fly the plane. These screens are on 24 hours a day, 365 days a year, under challenging conditions such as frequent changes in air pressure, turbulence, and other adverse conditions and in temperatures ranging from 20° C (68°F) to over 60° C (140°F.) How many of those screens do you think broke down and had to be changed in the thirteen years we have had them on our planes? Not even one!

It Is the Fault of the Human

When everything started working as it should, but accidents continued to occur, we entered the second period – where evidence attributed most incidents and accidents to human error. It was easy and convenient to quickly name the culprit – that people simply couldn't keep up with technology. We hear that all the time nowadays, don't we?

In any field, technology advances by leaps and bounds, systems diversify, new things keep popping up, and investigators always chalk up mistakes to the human operator. But is it that simple?

In the new sophisticated modern airplanes, engineers automated many of the actions needed for the plane to take flight. Computers took control over a plane's operation, including small steps like connecting or disconnecting certain elements or systems. In response to the automation, the engineers removed two of the five seats in the flight deck. These individuals kept their right to be there: the commander, copilot, and the onboard engineer. The pilots and the plane's advanced systems eliminated the roles of the navigator, communications officer, and then, eventually, the onboard engineer.

Pilots received instructions and training to fly these new planes, of course, but cutting out three of the five people came with a price. It fell on these two superhuman pilots to pay it. On top of taking on full legal responsibility, pilots now also had to commit to memory heaps of comprehensive documentation, including thousands of parameters, emergency procedures, memory items, and navigation procedures. They learned an unfathomable number of details about all the drawers, plunges, indexes, pressures, temperatures, and hundreds of esoteric pieces of information like how the radar screen renders images, what a magnetron is, and how electron jets work, and so on.

When I did my Airbus 310 Type Rating course, I was already an instructor, and I had ten thousand hours on the Airbus 318/320 under my belt. At first, the A310 cockpit felt like a giant step back. There were extreme differences between the twenty-year-old A310 cockpit and the new Airbus 318/320.

The Airbus 310 has so many switches, a lot less automatization, smaller CRT screens – it felt like going back in time! I liked the plane itself, though; it was bigger – 164 tons, compared to the A318's 61 – and could fly greater distances, which made up for the inconvenience of having to learn how to fly an "older" plane.

When I opened the manuals, I went back twenty years to another training paradigm. I saw the functionality of the EFIS (Electronic Flight Instrument System), explained in 120 pages, including detailed descriptions of completely insignificant technical aspects over which the pilots have no control, but which they had to learn anyway. I realized how false the "humans can't keep up with technology" theory was.

The pilots' training was wrong because it was not humanly

possible to retain so much information and make good split-second decisions. Having to memorize hundreds of pages of systems and procedures and trying to shove tons of irrelevant technical tidbits into the poor pilots' heads had not been conducive to practical, systematic learning of how to operate an aircraft.

It's like giving someone a shiny new smartphone and telling them they will only be allowed to use it after memorizing two suitcases full of manuals on the gadget's inner workings. And they have to know it all by heart, including Chapter 65, "An In-Depth Examination of How an Image Is Rendered on a Touch Screen."

This type of training contributed to the perception of the plane as a capricious deity, flying somewhere overhead doing whatever it wants without the pilots having any control over it.

This system created neurotic pilots who, instead of reacting to whatever information was displayed to them on the cockpit screens, kept thinking about things like:

This type of training contributed to the perception of the plane as a capricious deity, flying somewhere overhead doing whatever it wants without the pilots having any control over it.

- The temperature in the duct
- The fire alarms
- The significance of warning lights
- The control networks
- The four computers
- etc.

Today we train beginners to get better acquainted with the flight deck – that interface between the plane and the pilot – and appropriately react to its signals. On the whole, we emphasize respecting *procedure* more than *knowing* every nook and cranny in the plane. The more experienced the pilots and the more they aspire to advance, the more versed they need to be.

Regular testing on the ground, in the simulator, and during the flight reassure both the airline and the aeronautic authorities that only professionals set foot inside the cockpit and that they are indeed prepared to handle any circumstance.

The old style of work – where people were mostly concerned with checking things off a list and passing on the responsibility to someone else – is counterproductive, and it has no place in a modern work environment.

No matter how complicated a job may be, there are always ways to prepare the "human factor" better. Passive box-ticking is not it, and that is why the paradigm has shifted to a more proactive approach.

It Is the Fault of the Airline

The old style of work – where people were mostly concerned with checking things off a list and passing on the responsibility to someone else – is counterproductive, and it has no place in a modern work environment.

The third period in the history of aviation accidents is the one we are in now. We've overcome most technological and human error-related issues. From a technical perspective, modern planes are exceptionally well built. Engines rarely fail, and even if they do, you'd have no trouble crossing the Atlantic Ocean on a single engine. Pilots are well prepared and frequently tested. We live in a time when accidents are admittedly a lot rarer. So, why aren't accidents a thing of the past?

We find that among the leading causes for them are decisions taken by airline management, like not allocating sufficient resources to essential sectors or saving on risk assessment and management services. Practically speaking, fierce competition and the need to turn a profit cause airlines to keep cutting costs in many sectors, including:

- Maintaining and inspecting aircraft
- Reducing the number of pilots to a minimum
- Maximizing their flying time
- Reducing personnel in sectors considered less critical

It seems, nowadays, that aeronautical authorities and international flight safety organizations are always at odds with airline management. Every time the managers let their "creativity" run wild, the authorities have to rein them in with all sorts of regulations like limitations, thresholds, responsibilities, as well as the means to monitor their enforcement.

Suppose you see a situation that, in your experience, could lead to a tragic accident. The best solution is to frequently communicate what bothers you and insist on things that help you maintain your personal safety and that of others around you. Aim to express your concerns as calmly, rationally, concisely, and as neutrally as possible.

I am not suggesting you blindly accept whatever happens, or that managers are always right. Doing that is a surefire way to lose yourself. You've probably met people who started their professional life full of energy and initiative but now resign themselves to bitterness or cold self-servitude in which they don't lift a finger unless there's something in it for them.

What's Your Attitude?

In the previous chapter, we addressed the subject of attitude. We're going to expand it a bit now because attitude makes all the difference. We can influence it for better or worse through a submissive, aggressive, or assertive approach, depending on what we decide.

Consider what happened to an Air Florida flight on January 13, 1982. The Boeing (737-222) had to be de-iced at Washington National Airport in Arlington, Virginia. Even after de-icing, the plane had trouble moving away from the gate due to ice. While it sat on the airport's only open runway for 45 minutes, it accumulated more ice. The pilot made the decision to not return for more de-icing, and to not turn on the plane's own de-icing system.

The CVR revealed the copilot told the pilot, "It's a losing battle trying to de-ice these things. It gives you a false sense of security. That's all it does." Thirty seconds after reaching the end of the runway, the plane hit the 14th Street Bridge over the Potomac River, striking cars, before plunging into the icy river. Seventy-three people and four motorists died.[1]

Airline safety experts assert this crash is an example of a submissive approach by the copilot, who could have suggested a different sequence of events. Imagine the cockpit conversations over the years. Which discussions resulted in death and which avoided tragedy? See Chapter 8 for the story of a plane crash that occurred, in part, because of miscommunication.

Consider this. How many people are alive today:

- Because a pilot or copilot spoke up instead of being quiet and submissive?
- Because the plane's WARNING lights came on?
- Because the pilot kept their cool and remained assertive and communicative?

By choosing the right attitude every time and leading by example, you can influence the attitude of those around you.

Apart from a minimal amount of flight hours, pilots who wish to become commanders receive an evaluation on three key criteria: knowledge, skill (ability), and attitude. The first two are considered fundamental technical aptitudes that are relatively simple to evaluate. The third criteria is harder to measure but is nonetheless essential.

By choosing the right attitude every time and leading by example, you can influence the attitude of those around you.

Knowledge

Candidate pilots must exhibit a high level of familiarity with aeronautic legislation, air navigation, aerodynamics, aeronautical meteorology, aircraft communications, the plane systems, and many more aspects. These are all available for study, and that is, again, relatively simple: the more you want to know, the more you read.

Skill

Your skills as a pilot grow with experience, so the more you repeat the maneuvers, the better you get. Apart from certain physical limitations, or certain people who simply do not have the predisposition, anyone can learn to fly. It takes minimal attention span and a bit of discipline, but in theory, anyone can fly a small recreational plane.

But you can't fake a smooth landing; either you can do it, or you can't. It immediately shows, and that is why beginner pilots are very concerned with this particular skill. But I'm more worried about pilots who don't communicate correctly in-flight or don't know the procedures as well as they should, much more than I am about how smooth their landing is. I even have a saying: I can take my teenage son and make him land a plane a hundred times until he nails it, but that doesn't make him a good pilot. That requires a different set of skills.

Flight skills are also pretty easy to evaluate because we have checklists for everything: how the pilots apply their knowledge, how they communicate with air control or their copilot, how they maneuver the plane in the air, and how they land.

One can also learn correct communication and perfect it through repetition until it is second nature. That is why we dedicate a significant portion of this book to communication because it is essential to everyone: a single person, family, company, and even an entire community.

Attitude

The hardest thing to evaluate is someone's attitude. Despite a whole mechanism of evaluation and control, this aspect still proves quite tricky.

Attitude is the most critical element, the magnifying glass through which we inspect a professional.

It is not merely the cherry on a cake made of years of study and hard work; it is the very thing that makes the cake rise. It depends greatly on your environment, where and how you grew up, first at home, then in formal education, your culture, and your professional training. Knowledge and skills need a base, a foundation. That foundation is a correct attitude towards others.

Attitude is the most critical element, the magnifying glass through which we inspect a professional.

Have you ever found yourself being submissive or aggressive in the workplace? What about outside of your professional life? Have you ever held your tongue, knowing full well that things would have a less than favorable outcome, out of respect or fear of people around you? Recall the people who were attacked because they asked someone without a mask to put one on during the Covid pandemic.

As a leader, do you encourage your team members to speak up and feel free to give each other feedback? To you?

Commanders are the most experienced member of the team, the leaders. They are the most prepared and have the necessary knowledge and skills to guarantee a smooth landing every time. Of course, this status may sometimes lead to inappropriate attitudes such as arrogance. In the absence of *checks and balances* and no option to contest the leadership, it is up to the leaders to establish ways to hold themselves accountable.

The simplest way to do that is to acknowledge that you're human and that no matter how experienced you are, you're going to make mistakes. There will be things you'll miss, details you won't be able to see, regardless of how good you are or how many times you've done it. Wouldn't it be better if you had someone you could trust to tell you when something is amiss?

For all those reasons, my response to my copilot on my flight to Istanbul couldn't have been anything but "correcting." No aggressiveness, no excuses, no resentment – just a prompt "correcting." And let me tell you something: I was nothing but glad to have had that exchange because I knew that my response reassured my young copilot of his competence. Today, he is a commander himself.

Be a good leader, communicate assertively, listen to the people around you, and do your best to contribute to their development.

Part Two | Lead Responsibly

4 How Do You Build an Airplane?

You can think of your role as a leader as a little question mark in the upper tip of an equilateral triangle. Here is the story of that triangle.

The Critical Importance of Design

After seventeen years at the company and 10,000 flight hours under my belt, I became a student again. I went back to ground training to learn how to fly an A310, and I was about to get into the oldest flight simulator I had ever seen. It wasn't easy to find an instructor for me, but the guys at the training center in Frankfurt managed to bring in a retiree who still had a valid TRI license. My relationship with the plane that would become the love of my professional life, the Airbus 310, did not set off on the right foot; I was in an "ancient" plane, an "ancient" simulator, and had an "ancient" instructor to match.

The A310 was the first wide-body plane for two pilots certified to fly over long stretches of uninhabited areas (oceans, deserts, and jungles) on two engines. Until then, the industry standard was to use four-engine planes for such long hauls.

The certification for the ETOPS (Extended Twin Operations) forced manufacturers to introduce additional safety features that would secure a flight in case of engine failure. Airbus rose to the challenge and created one of the most legendary planes of the twentieth century. Its main, backup, and fail-safe system's redundancy level is so high that technology has only recently been able to catch up with it. Virtually all modern Airbus planes model the basic structure of the A310, with all the latest features.

I'll tell you an anecdote to give you a better idea of the significance of this airplane, which has become a favorite of everyone in the industry – engineers, flight attendants, and of course, pilots. I was with my crew on a technical stopover to refuel on the Island of Sal in Cape Verde. I had just passed through security, and I found myself standing behind a German crew from a big charter company. We looked somewhat exotic in our airline uniforms, a rare sight on the island, so the German captain approached me curiously and asked our company's name. I told him and showed him our plane.

Suddenly his face lit up. He ran to his bag and pulled out a tablet. He showed me the background on his screen: an image of an A310, painted in a German airline's colors. He beamed at me and told me that although he and his crew had flown many other types of planes, the A310 still had a special place in their hearts.

How Are Planes Built?

Before the first simulator session in Frankfurt, in the first hour of the briefing, the instructor asked us if we knew how planes were built. We exchanged confused looks – of course we knew! But we couldn't figure out what that had to do with any of the training that we were supposed to be doing.

The instructor drew a long horizontal line at the bottom of the board. "Building an airplane starts with an idea," he said, "a market survey. Let's say research shows demand for a 100-seater with two jet engines with a flight time of three hours." He wrote those requirements on the right tip of the line. "If we know how many people the plane has to seat, we know what size the fuselage has to be to fit the passenger cabin and the luggage hold." He drew a second horizontal line above the first one, a little shorter at both ends. On the right, he wrote, "fuselage." "Now that we know the approximate weight of the plane, we can choose the right type of engine." He wrote "engines" at the right tip of a third horizontal line above the second one, a little shorter on both sides.

"Of course, we know how much fuel a three-hour flight requires, so we can add that, the reserve fuel, and the weight of the wings themselves to the calculation." He labeled the fourth horizontal line, again shorter than its predecessors on both sides, "wings and fuel reserve." Then he drew some more lines: "landing gear," "hydraulic system," "electrical system," "pressurization," and so on.

The first tier at the base of the triangle represents the design and construction phase of making a plane, including various tests and computer simulations, and everything else until the test pilots get the prototype.

The lines formed a trapeze, the base of an equilateral triangle in the making. Until that point, it was more of a thought experiment, fitting together all the systems that keep the aircraft safe and functional.

The first tier at the base of the triangle represents the design and construction phase of making a plane, including various tests and computer simulations, and everything else until the test pilots get the prototype.

Test, Test, Test

Testing an aircraft is hard, painstaking work that takes years because you have to test all its different functions and systems, its behavior in different scenarios, and other elements.

It starts with getting the plane onto the runway to inspect and document all the engines' working parameters. The testing process puts the plane through various regimens, recording the plane's maneuverability on the ground and using its brakes at different speeds. If anything is less than perfect at that stage – if the engineers detect a malfunction or reduced performance in any of the systems – sometimes you can fix them on the spot by replacing certain parts. But in other situations, you can't.

You've heard this kind of announcement when you are a passenger boarded at the gate and awaiting the move onto the runway. You notice you are waiting longer than normal to push off. Then you hear the dreaded announcement. "This is your captain speaking. We saw a light on the flight desk. Our engineers determined we cannot take off with this issue, and we're going to need to switch planes." You groan.

If the engineers discover the brakes overheat to the point where you need to delay the takeoff to let them cool after a landing, you might try to replace the brake pads with stronger ones or install a fan on the wheels to cool the brakes.

In the classroom, the instructor drew a new line, the first in the new tier, and wrote "BRK Fan." That line represents a solution to a problem that the designers had not foreseen in the construction phase. It meant an additional cost for the extra materials and the added load on the plane.

The last scenario to be tested on the ground is an aborted takeoff and emergency braking. Again, the testers take notes and record videos of all the parameters. If they discover that some systems malfunction in any way, they will need to be changed – meaning a few extra lines on the triangle's testing tier. Step by step, panel by panel, strut by strut, and screw by screw, we get to the first take-off, which might take place months after the plane's first visit to the runway.

Several months of rigorous ground testing come down to this one moment of truth.

Every single person involved in the making of the plane can hardly wait for its first takeoff:

- The company's managers
- The designers who sketch the plane's schematics
- The engineers who run computer simulations
- The factory workers who assemble the plane

It's one thing to have a computer tell you that your plane can fly and quite another to see it with your own eyes.

Several months of rigorous ground testing come down to this one moment of truth.

The Stakes Are High

If the plane tanks or crashes, it becomes an expensive issue to resolve. Consider what occurred with the Boeing 737 Max, which crashed in 2018, killing 189 people, and in 2019, killing 157. In a settlement announced in 2021, Boeing agreed to pay $2.5 billion to settle a U.S. Justice Department investigation. Boeing admitted its employees misled regulators about the safety of its 737 Max aircraft.

With stakes this high, it's no wonder that no stone is left unturned in preparing for the first critical flight. A team of pilots and engineers, each with their own unique background and way of thinking, spends months poring over every possible scenario. Every person on the team has a backup, a "fresh pair of eyes," whose job is to monitor the flight parameters closely and, more importantly, act as a stand-in if one is needed.

Instead of actual passengers, the plane is fitted with barrel-like containers that can hold different water quantities so the testers can observe its behavior at different weight loads and weight distribution.

When it's doing its usual airline routes, that type of plane won't always be fully booked, and the pilots need to know what settings and speeds to use at takeoff in relation to its weight. The plane will take off on different runways, at different elevations, and at varying temperatures and atmospheric pressures.

By the time regulators clear a plane for commercial use, it has already had thousands of flight hours, testing out all its different systems in a myriad of conditions that mimic its intended usage.

The First Airbus 380 Flight

One of the most memorable moments in recent aviation history was the launch of the Airbus 380, the impressive European double-decker, the largest passenger plane in the world. At least 50,000 people came to Toulouse on the morning of April 27th, 2005, to bear witness to that one-of-a-kind giant taking to the air for the first time.

The takeoff was broadcast live worldwide, including on a gigantic screen in Toulouse's main square. Regardless of where they were watching the takeoff – near the runway, in France, or even on television – everyone was rooting for the leviathan to take to the sky.

The crew was also prepared in case the calculations on paper did not match reality.

All crew members wore parachutes on their backs; they didn't have them stowed away somewhere on the plane.

The crew also had a special handrail mounted on the nearest emergency exit for quick evacuation if necessary. Fortunately, the plan went off without a hitch, and the plane landed safely after four hours in the air. For the flight's entire duration, the plane's trajectory and other data were transmitted live for the experts on the ground. Airbus received congratulations from everyone, including its biggest rival across the pond, Boeing.

The buzz surrounding the A380 culminated two and a half years later, on October 25th, 2007, when the new Airbus completed its inaugural flight with Singapore Airlines, bearing the symbolic number SQ 380, from Singapore to Sydney, with 470 passengers and 30 crew members on board. Again, thousands of people swarmed the two airports to get a good look and snap a few pictures of the new plane.

All crew members wore parachutes on their backs; they didn't have them stowed away somewhere on the plane.

The tickets were put up for auction, and the first two First Class seats on its outbound leg sold for a whopping $100,380. The auction started at $380. If you had been willing to settle for an economy seat, you would have paid the "bargain" price of $7,500. On average, the first A380 passengers paid *ten times* the price of a regular ticket. All the proceeds from the ticket sales for the A380's inaugural flight went to charity.

I haven't been lucky enough to test a brand-new aircraft, but I have served as a test pilot for planes that had come back from extensive technical maintenance. These routine checkups must be done on all planes every few years or after a certain number of flight hours.

The Importance of Inspection

Sometimes, after a long time between inspections, it is necessary to take apart the plane and separately examine every component: landing gear, engines, electrical system, generators, and other features. The plane becomes a hollow carcass; the engineers inspect its hidden cavities for cracks, using an aeronautical endoscope. They replace every cable, rod, and strut that shows a hint of wear or corrosion. Putting this gigantic puzzle back together is an arduous process, followed by an equally meticulous inspection of the entire plane.

> In the history of modern aviation, obstruction or blockage of the pitot tubes, like leftover adhesive tape after a paint job, has caused several serious accidents.

I have flown several planes that came back from servicing, and I can tell you that the ground checklist alone takes almost two hours to complete. I once even found a strip of protective tape on one of the pitot tubes. A team of painters had painted it, and it was so transparent that none of the technical teams that had inspected the plane noticed it before they handed it to me.

Although it was invented over 250 years ago, in the early 18th century, before the first plane, a pitot tube is a vital sensor in modern aviation. It transmits the plane's airspeed to the flight instruments. Airspeed is a crucial bit of data.

In the history of modern aviation, obstruction or blockage of the pitot tubes, like leftover adhesive tape after a paint job, has caused several serious accidents.

Now you understand why we pilots are such sticklers for visual inspections of the plane's exterior before every takeoff, especially when it comes to those sensors!

The Test Flight and Nerves of Steel

For the test flight itself, you need three people in the cockpit – two test pilots and an onboard engineer – and at least two more people on the passenger cabin's technical team.

This type of flight requires an exclusive flight zone with no traffic, usually somewhere over the ocean or other unpopulated areas. The plane's testing consists of a progressive series of maneuvers done at different altitudes up to the maximum limit. For example, one maneuver starts with lowering the landing gear using the emergency system and retracting it back up normally. Then, the pilots stop and restart the engines one by one. The cabin undergoes controlled depressurization. This change results in timing how soon the oxygen masks drop from the overhead bins.

We test the plane at its highest speeds, with engines at full or reduced power, but the "crown jewel" or the "queen" of maneuvers is the almost vertical nosedive. We take the plane as high as it can go and then point its nose directly towards the ground, to the point where you can't even see the sky from any of the windows in the cockpit. The equalization of accelerations makes it feel like we're hovering midair, nose pointing to the ground.

This technique is how we test all of the plane's safety and protection features and let me tell you – it is anything but a dark cockpit in there. It's always a bit funny to see how the onboard engineers, who sit with us in the cockpit, react to these maneuvers, even though it's not their first rodeo, and they know exactly what's going to happen. One of the older engineers even tried to convince me once not to turn off the second engine because "we have already made the other one restart, so we know the system works just fine."

I understand them – I wouldn't feel comfortable either, being a mere spectator with zero control over the aircraft.

Imagine how much trust must exist between the pilots and the technical team for them all to get on a plane together, knowing that only a few days ago, it was in pieces.

Pilots may receive all the credit, but you should know that a flight's success is due in no small part to the people who prepare the planes and take care of them. Suppose everything goes as planned, with no malfunctions that necessitate an emergency landing. In that case, a test flight can take up to four hours, during which all of the plane's data is meticulously recorded. Only after the flight parameters are analyzed on the ground and possibly adjusted for another technical test flight can the plane be put back in commercial use.

Imagine how much trust must exist between the pilots and the technical team for them all to get on a plane together, knowing that only a few days ago, it was in pieces.

But things are different when it's a brand-new plane. You're bound to come across some malfunctions, minor defects, and errors in the onboard computers over thousands of flight hours. Some of these may be adjusted or recalibrated. Still, it may be too late for others because the cost of direct or indirect modifications – including delays in the plane's delivery to the airline – could simply be too great.

Even if it's not perfect, the project moves forward with transparency, with remarks, notes, and warnings. For example, let's say we discover that some sensors have defects that may give incorrect commands to the aircraft's flight control surfaces. A system designed to help pilots keep the aircraft safe is now limiting or even overwriting the pilot's commands. Until the sensor's software can be changed – which in itself is risky because it may cause a ripple effect in the design of the flight commands and create unforeseeable complications – the handiest solution is to inform the pilots of this defect and train them to work around it.

And so, with different remarks and notes, our plane construction triangle gets another line, which will consist of an entry in the QRH (Quick Reference Handbook) – a manual that all pilots carry and refer to when required.

Slowly but surely, the equilateral triangle already develops two tiers: at the base, we have concept, design, and construction. In addition, we have real-life testing before the plane is cleared for mass production. What else could we add to the triangle? There is still plenty of room at the top.

It is now time for another drawing, if you will. Please draw a big equilateral triangle, like an Egyptian pyramid that you would see from a distance. Split it in three horizontal layers of more or less equal height. Next to the layer at the bottom, please write Design & Construction. Next to the middle one, please write Testing. Next to the top one, please write Commercial Use.

In this chapter we talked about the many horizontal lines that represent different things. Please draw them, inside the first two layers. But be sure to leave the top third empty at this stage. You'll discover below the meaning of that. That empty, smaller triangle at the top of the big one is a visual way to express what your role as a leader is.

Ready to Roll

The last tier represents the transition to commercial use. The plane has now been built and tested; it has all the necessary certifications and authorizations, and it is safe for use by clients and passengers. Still, there's always room for improvement.

The first airline to operate a new type of plane is called a launch customer. Along with the prestige of innovation, being a launch customer means taking on the risks and responsibilities of using and continuously improving cutting edge technology, a burden they share with the manufacturer. Do the lithium batteries overheat on long hauls? It might mean going back to the drawing board and tinkering with the electrical system (maybe using smaller batteries but in larger quantities), but it's not likely.

The manufacturer will probably issue warnings recommending the use of that specific type of airplane for shorter distances. But that's no reason to call off the project. The manufacturer might even develop some modifications to the cooling system, like expanding it, which will undoubtedly mean further delays that would ground the new planes and leave passengers dissatisfied with the changes to their itineraries. Either way, our triangle now has a "batteries" line on it.

Suppose two of the three computers that manage data about speed, pressure, temperature, and other aerodynamic information freeze in the same conditions, which leads to an error in the central control system. This problem creates another line, another warning, another exercise to add to the simulator until a backup program indicating the speed and the angle of attack can be designed, written, and thoroughly tested.

Airlines all over the world already buy and use a company's planes. Every month, more planes of this type enter the market. That means more flight hours, which can mean additional lines added to the triangle's top tier, each one getting us one step closer to perfection.

The aviation community is very close-knit – airlines and plane manufacturers tend to have very close relationships. Similarly, there is a strong bond between airlines and aeronautical authorities, who oversee the airlines' operations. Information gets around fast because it is a vital field in which each pilot's individual experience in flying this or that plane counts a lot. Our triangle is now almost full. Even years after the launch of a plane model, experts continue to add lines to the third tier of the triangle.

Today, when I teach, I also draw the Frankfurt instructor's triangle for my students. Knowing the plane so well, we can fill the triangle with data that is relevant to us. The lines in all three tiers have different names. Some are things we contributed ourselves; others we only read about a week after their addition. I always make a point of leaving the tip of the triangle empty, and I draw a question mark there.

That little empty triangle with the question mark in it is one of the main reasons you need a commander, and through that same tiny triangle, you can define your role as a leader. They hired you to lead. If you run your own company – that area of uncertainty is exactly where you're needed the most.

It is like a warning – no matter how many hours of flight you have on a plane or how experienced you are in general, surprises can still sneak up on you at any time.

Your Role as a Leader

To wrap up this first chapter of the second part of the book, here is some food for thought. Here are nine ways in which the pilots' triangle and your triangle as a leader are alike.

1. Computers and Manuals Could Never Fill the Empty Tip of the Triangle

Despite the high level of automation in modern planes, a self-piloting aircraft is still a distant dream.

A. You would struggle to find passengers who would want to get on a pilotless plane.
B. If you do manage to find a few willing daredevils, we still can't account for every possible scenario with a program, no matter how many "If x then y" statements we put in it.

One cannot handle that tiny empty space at the tip of the triangle without a great deal of experience, extensive training, good judgment, and human values. Even today, a flight's critical moments – mainly takeoff and landing – are done manually. Theoretically, however, the autopilot could execute them.

Your role as a leader is similar. If your triangle was full 100% – that is, if you could write procedures for everything your team does, no one would need you. It would be enough to assign one person to 100 or 200 employees, whose sole job would be to turn off the lights at the end of the day when everyone goes home. Simply put, your primary role is to:

Your employees want to know that whoever is at the helm can make good decisions and keep them in mind when they do.

- Handle uncertainty
- Motivate your people
- Make them care about their workplace
- Reassure them of their future in it

Your employees want to know that whoever is at the helm can make good decisions and keep them in mind when they do.

You can't have that kind of relationship with a computer.

2. You Never Start with a Clean Slate

Leaders taking their first steps "inherit" something. In a big company, this usually means people, practices, and other "legacy features" left behind by the previous boss. Leaders walk into the group's and the company's work dynamics, their relations with the clientele and other departments, the office plan, the salaries, etc.

If you're starting your own company, the "inheritance" is much more modest, but it still exists.

Your milieu includes all of your accumulated experience – from your former bosses, your studies, or your own life – as well as the habits your team members bring to the table.

When you become a leader, you're already in a pre-defined

setup. That is your starting point. In the cockpit, the screens and the controls have a particular arrangement. The Airbus 320 offers more agility, while the Airbus 310 handles a bit differently.

In the event of an incident or accident, commanders never blame it on the cockpit's layout or the plane's previously known, albeit problematic, issues. Why are managers so quick to point the finger at an existing setup, a "legacy," when things don't work? It is up to managers to tackle the problems and to correct them. These accusations are no way to lead. It strips away your credibility, and pretty soon, you'll be out of a job, too.

> If you're starting your own company, the "inheritance" is much more modest, but it still exists.

3. You Can't Travel Back in Time, You Have to Look to the Future

Most of the time, the correct solution is not to hit "undo" on an existing system or optimize a faulty one, thinking that everything will be OK if we just stick it out. If your offices are small and overcrowded, the solution is not necessarily to look for someplace bigger. Maybe it would suit you more to not have offices at all, only a flexible space for meetings, and have your employees work from home, your clients' offices, their favorite coffee shop, or even a park bench.

If we look at industries that have changed drastically, we see that most often, the change came not from optimization but from a completely new approach. I'm sure we can all think of at least a few examples. Consider what Steve Jobs did for phones (iPhones), music players (iPods), and digital books in the form of iBooks on iPads. The key takeaway here is that the change might not have come from the field's corporate moguls, but from outside players, underdogs, to whom no one gave a second thought in the beginning. Often, big corporations are too busy looking to the past, trying to save a buck or two here and there.

Building on the previous idea, you must choose: *Focus on the past or devote your energy to the future.*

4. You Can Make Your Team Better Every Year

Every pilot can add a horizontal line to the triangle and thus make their contribution to improvement. But that kind of chance only comes around once every few years because it's not every day that you find yourself in an unprecedented situation, something so atypical that it doesn't appear in any of the manuals, especially for planes that have been in use for a while.

Luckily, for people who don't spend every day in the sky, the chance to eliminate uncertainty and better their workplace presents itself much more often.

Luckily, for people who don't spend every day in the sky, the chance to eliminate uncertainty and better their workplace presents itself much more often.

The test of a leader is if they leave their team better than they found it. If you had to leave your team tomorrow, for whatever reason, how would they do? And we're not just looking at numbers, but at the team's potential to reach new heights in the future.

Many bosses squeeze their team for results so hard that the people have nothing left in them for the next quarter or the following year (when their so-called team leader will have moved on to greener pastures). These are the places that end up with the worst type of employees and in which professional growth is next to zero. Yeah, they delivered today, barely, but they won't be able to keep this up tomorrow or the day after that.

5. You Don't Have to Do It All Alone

Every leader has their own tip of the triangle and their own question mark. In aviation, information gets around very quickly; a problem that a French pilot has today will be known to pilots in other countries within weeks, if not days, along with its solution. Pilots all over the world receive training on how to handle problems that once led to fatal crashes. The passengers' safety and the successful landing of every plane are of the utmost importance to pilots, and that is why they are so open to sharing their knowledge with their colleagues and why they're never too shy to ask.

But outside of aviation, how open are leaders to talking to others about their work? And I don't just mean their successes and big plans, but also their failures and the problems they're facing, the CAUTION and WARNING lights in their cockpit. If you have a few work confidants with whom you can have an open, honest discussion – more in-depth than the usual "everything is A-OK, we'll exceed our annual expectations this year" – you're on the right track. The open sharing in masterminds for C Suite level leaders can be quite effective in getting objective suggestions for tackling problems.

6. That Tiny Empty Triangle Tip Should Be Even Tinier

In aviation, the empty space at the tip of the triangle can only shrink if every new special case is well documented and communicated to anyone who could use the information. We don't want pilots to keep their know-how to themselves or as an informal exchange between colleagues. We want everyone to be prepared and to not have to reinvent the wheel every time there is a problem. In our occupation, having to reinvent the wheel can cost both human lives and a great deal of money.

How much of the know-how in your company or team gets

shared as more than a water cooler chat? If all the employees relocate to the other side of the world tomorrow – what will you do then? The chances of that happening any time soon are slim, but in today's reality, when employees spend less and less time at a workplace than previous generations, anyone might leave at any moment. As a leader, you can more easily ensure continuity and keep delivering good results if the knowledge is well documented and easily accessible.

A handy trick to have up your sleeve as a leader is to assign responsibilities according to your team members' preferences and play to their strengths.

7. Some People Prefer Small Question Marks, Others Like a Challenge

A new plane that just hit the market, like the 737 Max, means more stress for the crew on its first few flights than on a good old dependable Airbus 310, whose triangle is full up almost to the top.

You can say the same about the responsibilities you assign to your people. Some of them hold their own under pressure, but others might not handle great uncertainty very well.

A handy trick to have up your sleeve as a leader is to assign responsibilities according to your team members' preferences and play to their strengths.

Any leader can do that, at least to some extent.

8. Your Career Is Always a Work in Progress

You already have one of the critical characteristics of a true leader: the belief that there's always room for improvement, that you can always optimize the way you do things, and get a better understanding of your field, your people, and your projects. Though it would be hard to lead without that quality, some leaders stop learning at some point.

Suppose we are comfortable in our leadership skills and the company is making great progress. Just when we think the question mark is about to disappear, often we're the ones who look for the next challenge. For some in the C Suite, it means looking for the next bigger opportunity. The median tenure for CEOs at large-cap (S & P 500) companies has dropped over the decades. A 2018 research study showed the median tenure was 5 years at the end of 2017.[2]

I speak from experience when it comes to changes. The first plane I ever flew was an Antonov AN24. After that, I flew an ATR 42/72. Then I switched to an Airbus 318/320, and ultimately, I got certified on the Airbus 310, which I have been flying for years and would gladly continue to do so. Perhaps one day, I'll look for the next challenge.

9. Aviation Is Magic. Is There Something Exceptional in Your Team?

Why would anyone pay ten times the ticket price, like the passengers on the A380's inaugural flight? It's not an everyday occurrence, but from time to time, people are willing to spend more. And even if the flight itself is not unique, there are special occasions. For instance, imagine a kid's first time on a plane, when they're so excited and curious they don't even know where to look first, much less stay in their seat; or imagine the first time a grandparent sets foot on an aircraft, not believing that they lived long enough to experience such a miracle.

There is also always the off-chance you will get a surprise upgrade on a long-haul flight, and as you make your way to your new seat, you are filled with newfound confidence, or maybe, on the contrary, you feel more sheepish than usual.

These experiences are priceless, and people would be happy to have them in the workplace as well. If you're thinking, "Hmm… that's all very well, but I don't have an Airbus with which to bewitch my employees," you're right. Sometimes, though, a little goes a long way: even a simple "thank you" for something one of your employees didn't think anyone would notice or other thoughtful gestures can breed trust, little by little, line by line, day by day.

To sum up, here's a little challenge for you: Every one of the similarities I've listed included suggestions you could implement. Some were explicit; others you'll only find between the lines. If you earned a point for every one of those that you already do, plus a bonus point for taking on the challenge – would you score a ten? Probably not, because it's pretty hard. But what is your score? And in a year, if you set out to grow as a leader – how much would you score then?

5 | A New Crew Every Day

How exactly do you establish leadership? When people look around for a leader, how do you convince them that you're the person to follow? What can you do to prove your worth – beyond what's on your calling card or the number of stripes on your shoulder strap – to unite people around you and make them want to listen?

What Makes a Leader?

I'm going to list five traits that make a leader. Of course, there are more, but these are the five essential traits without which your team will think less and less of you with each passing day. If you want to reaffirm your role as a leader in a healthy and relevant way, you must demonstrate these five traits to your people as soon and as often as possible.

This chapter's title refers to a fact of life in any major airline: Every day, you fly with a different crew. In the world's largest airlines, with fleets of hundreds of planes, a captain could go a year without having the same copilot twice. What do you think the chances are of flying with the same crew two flights in a row? Considering all this, even though your rank is clearly displayed on your shoulders, it cannot replace true leadership skills.

You're the one who has to instill trust in your people.

That is exactly what this chapter is all about.

In your daily life, at work, in sports, or other areas of your life, you probably mostly deal with the same people. These traits are just as important, if not more so because inconsistency in presenting them would raise many questions regarding your ability to lead.

One small caveat: What I'm about to tell you does not replace the age-old debate on what it takes to be a leader, from the poetic notion that a true leader "has a vision" to the tiresome "the team as a whole is greater than the sum of its parts." These debates may go on forever – and they will – and they are valuable because, in the end, they give meaning to the title. But if you really want things to run smoothly with your team – today, tomorrow, and next year – there are five things that you simply can't do without, or you'll end up losing. You'll lose results, you'll lose people, you'll lose time, and you probably won't even realize what you've lost until it's too late. You may end up losing your job.

> You're the one who has to instill trust in your people.

5 Qualities of a Leader

1. You're the Boss – Act Like It

Before each mission, whether the flight is one hour or ten hours long, you meet the entire crew in the briefing room. Everyone sits at the same table: the two pilots, the commander and copilot, and the cabin crew – the flight attendants. If the flight is longer than 13 hours and meets a few other conditions – like the time of day during which the mission takes place – then at least two more pilots join the roster. They will take turns at the helm, following a strict schedule that includes actual flight time, observation from the jump seat (a foldable seat in the cockpit for people who are not actively operating the plane), and downtime in the crew's rest compartment, which is entirely separate from the passenger cabin.

The number of flight attendants also depends on several factors: the length of the flight, the number of passengers (no more than 50 passengers per flight attendant), and the number of emergency exits on that type of plane.

The Briefing's Purpose

In the briefing room, it is clear who the commander, copilot, and chief purser are. We all have a distinct job description, we all know what we have to do, and we all know the chain of command should one of the crew members become incapacitated.

As part of the briefing, the commander informs the crew of

- The number of passengers
- Special goods in the cargo hold (which might include coffins, live animals, inflammable substances, lithium-ion batteries and so on)
- The length of the flight
- The expected weather
- The aircraft's taxi time
- Minor defects in the plane that may or may not affect the flight – the CAUTION lights

We do all these things for one straightforward reason: the whole crew needs to be on the same page, so everyone knows what to expect.

We also do a quick run-through of emergencies and their respective standard calls. Sometimes we don't have much warning, and there is simply no time to explain, so communication needs to be efficient. That is why we decide in advance how to code the communication for every eventuality. We discuss aborting takeoff to emergency evacuation and even extreme situations like a hijacking or a suspected bomb on board.

As part of the briefing, the commander might also quiz the crew, ask them some quick questions to make sure that everyone knows their role in a scenario, as a rehearsal.

After the flight attendants leave, the two pilots stay behind to discuss the flight's technical details and make some calculations to communicate the fuel details to the dispatcher: how much they need to refuel, how much they will consume, and possible tweaks to the flight plan. If everything is OK and there are no operating restrictions, the commander will ask, "What do you want to do?" This question refers to who goes first as Pilot Flying and who goes first as Pilot Monitoring. An even shorter version of this would be "outbound or inbound?" In the briefing room, they will decide who will be the PF and the PM.

As part of the briefing, the commander might also quiz the crew, ask them some quick questions to make sure that everyone knows their role in a scenario, as a rehearsal.

Now imagine the impression you would make as a commander if you came into the briefing anxious about the flight's length, the expected weather conditions, or any other factor. Suppose you started the meeting with, "Looks like we're gonna have a rough ride today; I hope we can handle it. I wonder what we should do." Or you skipped over essential parts of the briefing, and someone had to point out the fact that you had left some things out.

I make it a habit of being the first person in the briefing room, at least a few minutes before the rest of the crew. That way, I can familiarize myself with all the information and aspects of that flight. In other words – I do my own briefing before the briefing, so I always have a handle on everything.

Remember it is the first impression people have of you, and you would be doing a great disservice – both to yourself and your team – if you came unprepared or unsure of yourself, not to mention hurting your chances of completing the task successfully.

"Act as if you own the place" is the expression I'd use to describe the type of self-confidence you need.

Do everything you need to do to have control of the situation. Sure, it might be hard at first, but you have to be ready. Do your reading, listen to your favorite music beforehand, and make sure you show your confidence in others, as well.

"Act as if you own the place" is the expression I'd use to describe the type of self-confidence you need.

Have you ever heard of a leader saying, "It's gonna get hard. Real hard. I have no idea what we're gonna do. Follow me!" and have people follow? I don't think so.

2. Treat Everyone with Respect

Few things destroy trust in a leader like arrogance. A leader can be very self-assured while also convincing their team that they can move mountains. But in today's work culture or political atmosphere, having a leader disrespect some people on their team whose job they consider less critical can quickly turn things sour for everyone.

Flight Attendants

Unfortunately, I sometimes see commanders and even passengers treat flight attendants without the respect they deserve. Let me tell you something about flight attendants – or stewards as they're sometimes called. As a passenger, you've met them. They represent a diversity of races, sexes, and ages. They're the ones who greet you aboard the plane, show you to your seat and demonstrate what to do in case of emergency. If you're flying over water, they'll also show you how to use the life vest under your seat. During the flight, they serve you drinks, a snack, or maybe even a full meal – depending on how long the flight is and your type of ticket. Onboard service may occupy most of their time, but it is far from being the main reason they are there.

These professionals, my colleagues, are trained to provide first aid onboard. They are the best chance of survival an unconscious passenger has in the 15-20 minutes it would take me to safely land the plane at a nearby airport from an altitude of 12,000 meters. They are the ones who know how to use the halon fire extinguishers in case of an onboard fire, be it from a burning cigarette thrown in the bathroom trash can or from an electrical appliance's faulty battery.

But the level of their professionalism and dedication shines through in the darkest scenarios: an emergency evacuation, an inextinguishable engine fire, or uncontrollable smoke in the cabin. When panic strikes and passengers start running for their lives, some blocking the emergency exits in an attempt to take their things from the overhead compartments, or when they're too shocked to move, not knowing where to go – that's when the flight attendants come in. They keep their cool as their training kicks in, executing the plan they have made for themselves in their Silent Review, sitting in their seats doing what the procedure dictates for every takeoff and landing, and mentally going over what to do in case of an emergency.

They know how to handle themselves firmly, give the right orders, open the emergency exits, and usher the passengers towards safety. And if they only opened the doors and ran out to save their skins from the hell inside the plane, I don't think anyone could blame them – survival instincts can sometimes overpower any training or SOP – but the reality is often different. In most evacuation cases, we find fallen flight attendants right next to the emergency exit, a step away from clean air, a step away from life.

The explanation is simple and very human: Over the course of the flight, they've bonded with the passengers – smiling at the twins from row 9, joking with the elderly lady from 14E, chatting to the newlyweds in the back of the plane. So, when the smoke gets thick to the point when a single breath of it is enough to knock you out, and the temperature is unbearably high, these professionals try to get everyone off the plane – including the twins, the lovely lady, and the newlyweds. Every aviation accident victim list has at least one flight attendant on it, if not more. I see them as the equivalent of a firefighter running straight into the heart of the flames while everyone else is running away in the opposite direction.

Flight Attendants and Emergencies

In 1985, on a runway in Manchester, an explosion caused a massive fire in one of the engines, forcing the pilots to abort the takeoff and commence an emergency evacuation. Fifty-five people died of smoke inhalation, including two of the flight attendants whose bodies were found right next to the emergency exits. They received the Queen's Gallantry Medal posthumously, as did two other surviving members of the cabin crew, for their "coolness, outstanding courage, and devotion to duty. They remained at their posts and saved many lives." There were 82 survivors.

The same thing happened in Moscow in May 2019, when one of the 41 victims of a flaming plane evacuation was a flight attendant. Whenever there is a deadly incident such as this, we always find flight attendants among the victims. It's not because they couldn't have made it out in time but because they took their job very seriously. These are the same people that show you to your seat and serve you drinks, and they deserve all of our respect.

Consider the attention given to Captain Chesley Sullenberger, his First Officer Jeff Skiles, and the three flight attendants. Donna Dent, Sheila Dail, and Doreen Walsh had a combined flying experience of more than 95 years. They were on board an Airbus A320 that took off from LaGuardia on a frigid day in January 2009.

Two minutes into the flight, the airplane ran into a flock of Canadian geese. With both engines severely damaged, the plane lost its thrust, forcing Captain Sullenberger to land the plane on the Hudson River between New York City and New Jersey.

The flight attendants and the pilots helped the passengers get out of the water-filled cabin and out onto the wings, where local ferries and emergency responders rescued them from the icy water within minutes. One flight attendant was cut on her leg, and only 5 of the 150 passengers suffered more serious injuries than hypothermia.[3] Captain Sullenberger stayed on the plane until he was sure everyone was out of the cabin.

New York City Mayor Michael Bloomberg honored the pilots and flight attendants with the symbolic keys to the city. Rarely do pilots and flight attendants get into situations and survive to get this kind of attention. We think of notice as the day-to-day recognition for the efforts of the people on your team.

Imagine that you have to cross a chasm ten meters wide. You have a plank that's seven meters long, and someone else has a plank three meters long. Now, you can brag about having the longer plank all you want, but without the other one, you're never getting to the other side!

3. Listen First, and then Make an Educated Decision

We used to have commanders who would bark orders at us, question us about the plane as if in a pop quiz, and "punish" us if anything was not to their liking. They made sure we knew who the boss was.

The Results of Autocratic Rule

Consider how people react to the command-and-control leadership mode. This reaction is what I saw. The cockpit atmosphere was tense, and the communication was ice cold, stripped down to the bare necessities. These were different times, and it might have had something to do with our upbringing and culture.

Most of the time, it *wasn't* about technical failures or knowledge gaps but about the leadership's *inability* to listen, to use their subordinates' full potential, or to identify and delegate tasks.

This dynamic existed not only in "top" fields like aviation but other places like competitive sports and even school. It was customary for the boss to be a boss, big and strong, their actions never called into question. Their decision was law, even if they weren't always right. As I've demonstrated earlier in the book, the rules of aviation – its standards and procedures – were written in blood.

In those times, after every accident, you would look for its root cause.

Most of the time, it *wasn't* about technical failures or knowledge gaps but about the leadership's *inability* to listen, to use their subordinates' full potential, or to identify and delegate tasks.

Today, captains prefer to delegate to the copilot and use all of the plane's systems and automated functions (as long as they're working correctly, of course) to decrease the commander's workload, freeing them to deal with emergencies, and thus optimally supporting their decision-making process.

When we're talking about landing the plane with multiple malfunctions or in complicated conditions like strong winds, challenging weather, or on a river, the commander would be the one to man the controls, as both legislation and company policy puts the entire responsibility on their shoulders. But the rest of the time, the commander has all the necessary resources at their disposal, and it would be a shame if those resources went unused.

> Most of the time, it *wasn't* about technical failures or knowledge gaps but about the leadership's *inability* to listen, to use their subordinates' full potential, or to identify and delegate tasks.

Crew Resource Management

The three principles I've listed above come from CRM (Crew Resource Management), a concept created to reduce commander autocracy and breed assertiveness in copilots, especially in situations when the commander is about to make mistakes.

CRM has such a profound impact on the efficiency and safety of flying that it has become a part of aeronautical legislation worldwide and a mandatory part of pilot and aircrew training.

Even in flight simulator exams, CRM concepts serve as a magnifying glass to assess pilots' professional growth. This soft skill is the most crucial tool commanders have in their toolbox, but it's also the most difficult to teach in a classroom.

Let's look at a practical CRM example. What would you do if you were the commander, and what would you do if you were the copilot?

Do You Take off with Ice on the Plane?

When the air temperature drops below 5°C (41°F), a thin layer of ice forms on the wings, the rudders, and a plane's fuselage. When this coincides with other weather phenomena such as snow or freezing rain, this layer can become quite thick. Sometimes when we take the plane on a new mission, the transparent ice layer is so thick that the aircraft looks like a crystal sculpture or a gigantic jewel.

> CRM has such a profound impact on the efficiency and safety of flying that it has become a part of aeronautical legislation worldwide and a mandatory part of pilot and aircrew training.

Aside from the added weight (which can sometimes amount to several tons), any contamination or dirt on the plane's surface can compromise its aerodynamic performance. That is the last thing we want to happen at takeoff, one of the flight's critical stages.

Takeoff is one of the most intense moments for pilots due to:

- The plane's relatively low takeoff airspeed – around 250 kmh (155 mph)
- Its proximity to the ground
- The limited maneuvering space
- The airport's surroundings
- The wind
- Different weather conditions like gusts of wind (windshear or microburst)
- Limited time to react

(Recall in Chapter 1 I described the sterile cockpit concept of limiting all conversation to factors associated with takeoff so the pilots can completely concentrate on takeoff.)

Ice increases the plane's friction with the air, which causes greater resistance. Simultaneously, any contamination of the wings and other aerodynamic surfaces reduces their efficiency, diminishing lift and affecting the plane unexpectedly, making it much harder to control. The problem of ice or snow on the plane's surfaces is so serious that specific training is dedicated to it. Training involves everyone – from ground-handling crews who cover de-icing to the supervising team and to the pilots, who undergo special simulator exercises that focus on this issue. Every airline has an operation manual for de-icing that is updated every cold season, and all personnel get tested and certified for it. Nevertheless, ice is a persistent risk for crashes. An internet search reveals several stories of plane crashes due to ice.

At the ground inspection before takeoff, the commander decides if the plane needs to be de-iced. The pilot identifies which surfaces should be de-iced and with what kind of de-icing fluid, depending on how thick the ice is, the temperature outside, and the expected precipitation. The commander gives a ground agent a signed form, with which that agent communicates what needs to be done and later verifies if the de-icing meets the airline's standards.

I'm the Commander and I say "No"

A fellow commander decided the plane did not need de-icing on one of the flights because the ice layer was within the limits that allow takeoff. The copilot, on the other hand, thought the plane required de-icing. The commander stood his ground. After all, he was the commander, he had the final say, and his verdict was that the plane did not need to be de-iced.

Now I'll ask you what I asked so many times before throughout the book: take a moment to think about what you would have done had you been either of them. You can even do this exercise – like all the other exercises in this book – with your team and explore a few options and conclusions.

The commander and his copilot kept arguing, which obviously created some tension between them, further amplified by both of them calling the dispatcher to defend their argument. Ultimately, the company decided to de-ice the plane before takeoff. Imagine how strained the atmosphere in that cockpit must have been. I'm inclined to believe that the rest of the flight was a very dark cockpit, in more ways than one. When they got back, they both had to file a report explaining their viewpoint and discuss it with the company's head of flight operations.

I knew both of them quite well. The commander was an experienced pilot, on the brink of retirement. The copilot was well trained and about to make commander himself. I had the most interesting talk with the copilot. He described the whole incident in great detail:

1. The reasons he insisted on de-icing the plane, even though he knew the final decision was the commander's
2. The way he tried to talk his superior into seeing things his way
3. How he got to the point of calling the dispatcher

Knowing that he valued my professional opinion, after having spent many hours together in training and simulator sessions getting out of somewhat sticky situations, I asked him, "How would you have acted had I been the commander that day, and I had decided against de-icing?"

It was a difficult question because he considered de-icing necessary. He wasn't looking to fight with anyone. "What would you have done?" I insisted on asking.

"I would have reluctantly accepted your answer and agreed to take off, trusting your experience of many years over my judgment."

Then I posed another problematic question that caught him off guard: "What do you think *I* would have done had *you* insisted on de-icing the plane after I told you that I didn't think it was necessary?"

He shrugged; he didn't know what to say. My answer surprised him.

"I would have heard you out and that if I had seen that you were willing to go head-to-head with the boss over it, I would have agreed *without* further questions."

It's better to de-ice the plane if we're not 100% convinced that we don't have to. (Remember the story of the plane that did not go through de-icing and ended up in the Potomac River? See Chapter 3.)

Making that decision to de-ice would avoid all the tension in the cockpit, especially since this was the very beginning of a flight. We would have had to spend the next seven hours together in a room of four squared meters, 200 passengers in our care on the outbound leg, and 200 more on the way back. It's better to de-ice the plane and show mutual trust than to pull rank.

A commander is not always right; they have to be willing to listen and make the best use of their team.

And I am confident that once he made commander, he passed on that little lesson in leadership.

A commander is not always right; they have to be willing to listen and make the best use of their team.

Did You Understand Me?

It often happens that a pilot doesn't understand what the air traffic controllers say on the radio. The pilots repeat it back to make sure they've received the message, and if the repetition doesn't confirm the original message, the controller repeats it, or they switch to a clearer frequency.

Still, sometimes the message is repeated incorrectly because of distortion or radio jamming. In today's increasingly crowded airspace, with thousands of intersecting planes, the last thing that a controller wants to see on their screen is a plane headed towards the wrong altitude, runway, or airport. In such situations, when the pilots are not sure what was said, they ask the tower to repeat the message.

But in the world's busiest airports – like New York, London, or Paris – there is some pressure on the pilots to get on with it as quickly as possible. If every single plane asked the tower to repeat the message, it could easily lead – and I'm not exaggerating – to a collision.

Some pilots prefer not to ask to repeat the message and instead rely on what they think they heard. I've had it happen a few times when the copilot and I understood different things, and even when I was absolutely sure of what I'd heard, I preferred to listen to the message again to minimize the risks and eliminate any doubts my copilot might have had. After all, we're in the cockpit together, and I try not only to listen but also read between the lines, and only then make my decision while still maintaining a pleasant working environment.

Miscommunication causes more accidents and injuries than you can imagine – in every field.

4. Do Not Overlook Inappropriate Behavior, No Matter How Small

When I fly, I care about all aspects of the mission. I don't just lock myself in the cockpit to admire the view. Though the flight's safety is my primary concern, my involvement is not strictly limited to it. I care about how passengers feel, how comfortable they are, and how punctual we are. Due to security concerns, the interaction between the pilots and the passengers is minimal. The armored door to the cockpit is closed the moment the second boarding starts until the plane's landing and all the passengers disembark.

It might have been simpler for me to just go into the cockpit and mind my own business, ticking off another mission and logging some more flight hours, but I like my job too much to leave it at that, and every little detail counts.

I always ask the cabin crew, "How is it in the back?" Whether there are 48 or 270 passengers on board, I make sure the temperature is right; I try to avoid turbulence or stormy areas; and I make frequent announcements, so everyone knows how the flight is coming along.

One summer, I was flying the first in a series of charter flights to Tenerife. The plane was full of tourists on the way there, but we only had one passenger on the way back. I still welcomed her on board over the PA, I found out her name, and I told her all the flight details. When we landed, I thanked her for flying with us, which made the whole crew smile.

When security was not as strict as it is now, I even let passengers, including small children, into the cockpit, especially ones who fear flying or are ignorant about it and don't feel comfortable on a plane. Once they saw how in control we were and listened to some simple explanations about what they saw in the cockpit, many passengers told us that they weren't so afraid anymore.

When I say I care about every last detail of the mission, I also care about the rest of the crew being on the same page. It's no use investing in the newest, most advanced planes and the best pilots if, at boarding, the passengers meet a sulky flight attendant who couldn't care less. As I said, we form impressions at first contact, and that flight attendant is our interface with you, the passenger.

Let me tell you about the couple I met on one of my flights. I was seeing them off the plane after landing. The woman was pregnant, and it was obvious that she had been crying. Her husband was outraged, but he managed to keep a civilized tone as he told me what had happened. When descending to land, at around 3,300 meters (10,826 feet), the captain had turned on the seatbelt sign, signaling the flight attendants to start preparations for landing: securing the catering trolleys, checking that all the passengers are in their seats with their seatbelts fastened, and informing the commander: "Cabin secure for landing."

Without that report, the plane cannot land because landing without a fastened seat belt puts passengers at significant risk. Usually, after the commander turns on the seatbelt sign, there are about ten minutes until the plane touches the ground. In that interval, the pregnant lady asked the cabin crew if she could quickly use the restroom in the back, but they shut her down. Both the husband and the wife tried to get permission to assume legal responsibility for getting up and using the restroom, but the cabin crew held firm.

Both the flight attendant in the back and the Chief Purser kept quoting the regulations, insisting that no one can break these rules under any circumstances. The negotiations continued until the landing, which, on that particular flight, took place a good 15 minutes after I had turned on the seatbelt sign. The control tower made a last-minute change to the runway we were supposed to land on because the wind had changed direction, and we spent a few minutes reconfiguring the plane.

The husband complained about the cabin crew's cold, inhumane treatment of him and his wife. He said that they only needed a minute or two and that the landing took a long time, so his wife going to the bathroom couldn't have been that big of a problem.

Meanwhile, the cabin crew insisted that those were the regulations and that the passenger asked to use the restroom after I had turned on the seatbelt sign. So, who was in the right?

I apologized to the three passengers in the name of the entire crew for the discomfort, and I told the husband I admired his self-control, as it was obvious he was distraught. After everyone disembarked, I told the crew I wanted to do a de-briefing – a rare occurrence, not something I would ordinarily do. I closed the door to the plane so we wouldn't be disturbed by anyone from outside – the technicians and catering or cleaning crew who came to ready the aircraft for the next flight.

The Chief Purser already had the relevant page in the operation manual open. It plainly listed the steps for preparing the cabin for landing. In their explanations, he and his colleague somehow managed to blame me for turning on the seatbelt sign too early. They kept saying that they were only doing their job according to regulation, which clearly forbade anyone from getting up once the light was on.

I asked him questions.

- "How many flight hours have you had?" "Plenty," he said.
- "Why didn't you realize that we were still quite high up and that we were never going to land so fast that you couldn't let the poor woman use the bathroom?" No answer.
- "If, despite the cabin crew's response, the couple had gotten up and the woman had entered the bathroom anyway, what would you have done? Would you have forced a pregnant lady down on the aisle floor? Would you have smacked the husband on the head?" Again, no answer.
- "Why didn't you ask me on the intercom immediately after the couple turned to you?"

He couldn't answer any of the questions; he was just pleased to have done his job by the book. I told him I hoped he would reconsider his handling of the situation. I then asked if, when he got home at the end of the day, he would be pleased because the incident had left a bitter taste in my mouth. It wasn't easy to reconfigure the airplane at the last minute for the runway change, but we managed to do it discreetly with no sudden maneuvers that disturbed the passengers, and yet I couldn't consider that mission a success because by blindly following protocol, we had made a young mother-to-be cry.

5. Always Be Ready to Learn

I was in Ireland, helping a newly founded airline introduce ATR planes into their fleet. I had already had 2,500 flight hours under my belt at the time. I was a young, energetic captain, as I'm sure I still am now. It was one of my first flights there, and I didn't know anyone. Every pilot I had shared the cockpit with was a stranger to me, but we all spoke the same language, one you're already familiar with from earlier in the book – the language of SOPs.

On one of the flights, I flew with an Irish instructor, who was also responsible for checking me on that flight. He was tall and sturdy. He almost crushed the palm of my hand with his handshake, although he was over 60 at the time, recently retired from their national airline. He looked tough, old-school, an instructor-pilot with over 20,000 hours in the cockpit, mostly on massive, long-haul airplanes. We were going to fly together the entire day, from Dublin to Galway, three rounds – that's six takeoffs and six landings. It's a running gag in the industry that as a pilot, you should aim for the same number of landings as takeoffs.

Ireland is not known for sunny, windless blue skies, and we were looking at strong winds for the entire day, especially on the western coast. I was getting ready for a difficult day, in part because of the weather but also because of the instructor. The briefing went as usual, and it was obvious that the Irishman was used to commandeering long hauls. His briefing was short and to the point, no jibber-jabber or personal stuff, but at the same time, he wasn't distant or condescending. After the classic "outbound or inbound?" question, we decided he would fly the first leg to Galway.

The destination airport had a runway of only 1,289 meters (4,229 feet), and I was used to runways twice as long. As if that wasn't enough of a challenge, it was also very narrow – there was a big barn at one of the ends of the runway, which you had to "jump" over to make the landing. The other end was hidden behind the edge of a hill. But the cherry on top of that cake was the lateral wind, strong and relentless across the runway.

When we got to Galway, Captain "Grandpa" slammed the plane so hard on the ground that I thought it was going to break in half. It was the kind of landing where you have to remind yourself that any landing you manage to walk away from on your own two feet is a good one.

I didn't let myself say anything; I kept my poker face – we did have five more landings together that day – but I couldn't help but wonder how a pilot as experienced as he was could land the plane like that. We left for Dublin, and it was my turn to land. The runway was longer, true, but the lateral wind was just as merciless as in Galway, and even more turbulent because of the hills to the south. I had a perfect landing, smooth as butter. We both wore poker faces.

Next, we headed out to Galway again, where he made his second landing on the same runway with the same wind, again slamming the plane at the end of the runway. That was a bit much – I couldn't believe it! As I was waiting for the passengers to disembark, trying to regain my composure after the second rough landing, I heard the instructor say something. I asked him to repeat himself, convinced that he couldn't have said what I thought he'd said. He said, "Show me how to land the ATR," because clearly, he didn't know how to do it correctly, and he had to learn.

For a few good minutes, I wondered if I had misheard his heavy Irish accent. Maybe it was my upbringing or the culture I came from, but I couldn't quite understand a pilot ten times more experienced than I was asking me to show him how to land, but there he was, getting ready to be PM on the next two legs! And so, I landed the plane both in Dublin and in Galway, narrating and explaining all the maneuvers for kiss-landing an ATR without skimping on the details.

We approached Dublin for the last time that day, where he was going to land the plane. I was on the edge of my seat, curious to see how it would go. Lo and behold – it was perfect! Same difficult conditions, same brutal lateral wind, but he did it! He had taken in everything I said, perfectly blending the new information with his vast experience.

I came home completely wrecked, I lay across the bed, fully clothed, and I stared at the ceiling for quite a while. I was trying to process the beautiful leadership lesson I had just learned from one of the most experienced instructors and commanders I had ever met.

When was the last time you surprised your people the same way that Irish retiree left my mouth agape? If the answer is never – well, it's about time.

6 | 61 Signatures

The focus of this chapter is a word that we hear and use very often: *responsibility.* Let's explore what responsibility means for an aircraft commander, why it's one of the essential qualities of a leader, and what you can do to become a more responsible leader.

One of the first lessons in responsibility I ever got in my career in commercial aviation was when I first started working at the airline. I was a copilot on an AN24, and after ground training, simulator sessions, flight school, and a few months of cockpit supervision, I was finally certified to fly without instructors. I was about to take off on a short domestic flight to Baia Mare. The weather was good, what you would call *Calm, Cavok 1013.* When you have time, take a look at the glossary at the end of the book, where you'll find definitions of all the aviation terms I've used throughout the book.

It's More Than Kicking the Tires

When I got to the plane that day, the commander assigned the visual inspection of the plane's exterior to me, as part of the standard checks we do on the aircraft when we first receive it for a mission. I was very thorough in my inspection, and I discovered that one of the four tires of the main landing gear was damaged, with a visible lesion under the first tier of rubber.

To understand why that was important, you need to be a little more familiar with landing gear tires.

Most passenger airplanes land at a speed of about 220-240 kmh (136 to 149 mph).

No matter how smooth the landing is, when the tires first touch the concrete, they skid until they start rotating at the plane's speed. Imagine the wear on those things at first contact! That's why the wheels smoke upon landing – the rubber literally burns off.

Consequently, the tires wear out and need to get changed quite frequently. Of course, there is an acceptable level of wear with which you're still allowed to fly. Pilots can easily tell when the tires are too worn out because the manual describes in detail what the tire's surface should look like – the exact depth and width of the tears on the tread. You know the tire needs changing when its outer layers have worn out so much that you can see the concentric plies.

Most passenger airplanes land at a speed of about 220-240 kmh (136 to 149 mph).

Returning to the flight to Baia Mare, I immediately notified the commander that tire 1 was slightly worn out. He was in the cockpit, having a friendly chat with one of the ground technicians who gave us the plane and signed off on its condition. Before the commander could say anything, the ground mechanic, who was amused by my overzealousness, told him that he had also noticed the wear on the tire, but he hadn't thought it was a big deal since the plane would come back in two hours when it would then get changed. *The commander signed the logbook* and took out the station copy, which stays on the ground as proof that the captain has assumed responsibility for the plane and told me everything was right.

We took off towards Baia Mare with a plane full of passengers, the commander as the PF, while I was the PM, operating the radio and executing the commander's orders. Everything went fine, including the landing, but as the passengers disembarked, I noticed that the dispatchers who had guided us to the parking spot were a little agitated.

One of the wheels, No. 1 to be exact, the same one that had shown signs of wear and tear, had a *burst tire.*

We couldn't feel anything on the plane because the wheels are set in pairs, and each tire is specially reinforced to withstand landing even when the other tire is rendered unusable. *But what if they had both given out?* And what was the probability of the worn tire hitting the runway at exactly the spot where the lesion was?

From a technical standpoint, it wasn't a big deal – we had spares in the luggage hold, there was an onboard mechanic and a ground mechanic, and it only took a few minutes to change the tire, after which we took off back to Bucharest Băneasa Airport, our base.

One of the wheels, No. 1 to be exact, the same one that had shown signs of wear and tear, had a *burst tire.*

But when we landed there, we were welcomed by a small committee. They had heard about the incident. We had to fill out a report and explain what had happened, especially since the ground technician's report read, "The commander inspected the aircraft – see attached report signed by him – although the wear and tear on the tire had been reported." Nice, huh?

Accountability Never Ends

Out of curiosity, I counted the number of times I have to sign something on *every* flight, starting with reporting for duty.

Depending on the number of flight sections, the number of

landings, and the nature of the airports I land in, I sign about 30 different documents, with a total maximum of 61 signatures!

Most of these are liability forms – by signing, I confirm the aircraft's state when I first receive it, and I take responsibility for the plane itself and the load in the cargo hold, among other things. I like to joke that after I sign so many papers, the person I give them to almost skips away relieved – they're off the hook, no backsies! The commander signed off on it; he's gonna shut the door and take off any second now!

When I come to work, about an hour before takeoff, I have to sign a timesheet. From that moment on, my work clock starts ticking – my flight duty period – which is different from flight time. The airline and aeronautical authorities closely monitor these work and flight hours and my resting hours in between flights because exhaustion drastically diminishes pilots' cognitive capabilities and their reaction time.

Depending on the number of flight sections, the number of landings, and the nature of the airports I land in, I sign about 30 different documents, with a total maximum of 61 signatures!

That first signature means I legally declare that I am medically fit and that I do not suffer from anything that might affect my ability to operate an aircraft. I verify I am well-rested, and that I am not under the influence of any substance that would inhibit my performance. Airport authorities even do random check-ups on personnel on their way to the plane. They've asked me several times to take a breathalyzer test, other drug tests, and even a blood pressure test before getting on a plane. I wasn't the only one: Every crew member from any nationality who happened to be there at that moment, whether they were just getting in or about to leave, had to do them, too.

I remember one time when all crews in the Amsterdam airport

had to undergo a surprise drug test, and one American flight decided to land in Brussels instead of Amsterdam. This change of plans raised some eyebrows, and we all laughed about how much wine American crews were allowed on long hauls.

The Flight File: You Are Responsible

After the first signature, I take the flight file. This is what I am looking at.

1. I first look at the thick folder containing information about the current weather conditions and forecasts for the airports at takeoff, landing, and along the route. The report also includes specific weather phenomena that we may encounter, like the direction of the wind and areas with turbulence or icing.
2. Another report provides information about the airports or air spaces I will fly over, the NOTAMs (Notice to Airmen).
3. Yet another one lists details like the number of passengers, the cargo hold, parking position, and possible minor defects with which the plane can still take off.
4. Finally, we also find the flight plan – a summary of all the information, including the flight route. Almost all of these numbered sheets of paper include a space for the commander's signature, whether to attest to having read and taken the information into account or assume responsibility for the plane's final preparations.

After the briefing, the crew comes to the aircraft. The captain then checks the plane's logbook just to make sure that the previous commander hasn't logged any unaddressed problems. They also confirm that the maintenance engineer has signed the aircraft's release form, giving the OK to fly it, and then the commander visually inspects the plane's exterior.

If it is raining – in which case the plane still needs to be inspected – the delightful task falls to the copilot. Now that you've learned so much about the world of commercial aviation, allow me to reveal one of our unwritten rules, which we like to call the 10/90 rule: If there's a 10% chance of rain, there's a 90% chance the copilot is going to make the rounds.

If everything is as it should be, the commander signs the station copy – the form that declares the commander legally responsible for the aircraft from the moment they sign it. That form stays with the ground maintenance crew. Any malfunction or scratch detected after it's been signed is the responsibility of the last person who signed it.

I guarantee that pilots who sign their name on a piece of paper that makes them liable for a plane valued at tens or hundreds of millions of dollars leave no stone unturned in inspecting it beforehand.

I guarantee that pilots who sign their name on a piece of paper that makes them liable for a plane valued at tens or hundreds of millions of dollars leave no stone unturned in inspecting it beforehand.

As a flight instructor, I seek to develop that sense of responsibility in my students. For some, the burden is too great, but that's OK; they can choose not to become commanders. Others might not handle stress very well – the stress of bad weather or the stress of having to sign so many papers when there is a great risk of things not turning out the way they expected. Switching from the copilot's right hand side seat to the captain's seat on the left may seem like a small step to take – a single meter, in fact – but psychologically, it is a giant leap. It is no slight shift in attitude and an even more significant burden of responsibility.

I don't believe there is a universal method or a recipe for becoming a leader, but I do know that taking responsibility even when the consequences are less than desirable is definitely part of it.

We look for that ability in all commanders. Here's an excellent example of that.

The Buck Stops Here

I don't believe there is a universal method or a recipe for becoming a leader, but I do know that taking responsibility even when the consequences are less than desirable is definitely part of it.

When I was a green instructor at ATR, I also had administrative responsibilities, including analyzing and interpreting the decoded FDR (Flight Data Recorder). The FDR is a marvel of technology: It automatically records thousands of parameters from all the plane's systems during the flight. The software flags any deviation from the optimal parameters with a designation of 1 to 3, 1 being the smallest deviation in parameters or a slight deviation from a safe trajectory, 3 being deviations that endanger the flight.

For example, if a commander drives the plane too fast on the ground, the system will flag it. If the commander makes turns at that speed, the system will also record that as exceeded lateral accelerations, which is a separate parameter. Two "fouls" in one! If the plane's tilt is greater than the allowed maximum, it will automatically appear in the report. An alarm automatically comes on if the pilot runs the motors past their permissible operating limits.

This monitoring is true for any deviation or violation of imposed restrictions.

The flight "film" reads an image at intervals of one second, and if the investigated event is longer, the interval is four seconds. Newer digital FDRs can even create an animated simulation of the flight, including each pilot's movements and actions throughout the flight. Keeping in mind that the CVR also records and places all the sounds in the cockpit, you now understand how controlled our work environment is and that once we decipher the information, it leaves no room for doubt. Your actions are never invisible in a flight deck.

Speaking of the FDR and CVR, together they form what is popularly known as the plane's "black box" – though in reality there are two of them, and they're not black but bright orange, marked "Flight Recorder Do Not Open" on one side, and again in French on the other. They are incredibly sturdy, made to withstand ground impact at a speed of up to 500 kmh (310 mph).

Think of those crash test videos where cars get completely wrecked at speeds ten times slower.

These "black boxes" can bear temperatures of up to 1000° C (1,832° F), as well as endure complete submersion in water or other liquids in great depths, and they even have a beacon that self-activates in case of an accident.

Of course, we hope none of those features ever have to be put to the test. That is why we monitor everything and take immediate action even at the smallest transgression.

Usually, when the recorded deviations are no greater than 1 or 2, we check the respective flight's specific conditions and determine that the particular pilot's flying style did not cause them. If the deviations are not repetitive, we will mention them in the report with a recommendation that the respective pilot work on their plane-handling skills.

However, if the deviations are rated 3, the commander must

write a report explaining their actions. Usually, when these deviations occur, the commander has to have a conversation with someone higher up to determine if the deviation resulted from a knowledge gap, faulty training, not being disciplined, or some other reason, and there's a specific protocol for how to solve each one.

Is the Landing Gear Down?

> These "black boxes" can bear temperatures of up to 1000° C (1,832° F), as well as endure complete submersion in water or other liquids in great depths, and they even have a beacon that self-activates in case of an accident.

I had in front of me the deciphered FDR of a flight where the "landing gear not down" alarm sounded on landing, close to the ground. The alarm is a sign that the pilots had not executed the SOP and neglected to perform the pre-landing checklist. The pilot did not verify the landing gear's position, leaving it retracted – like in the Korean Air Jeju-Daegu flight from Chapter 3. However, in this instance, the commander was my former instructor and boss, a legend in his own right at the airline, extremely experienced in flying different planes. To me, he was not only a role model, but I also liked him as a person. I've had the pleasure of spending time with him outside of work, listening to him play the guitar or read some of his poetry.

But on that day, I was put in the awkward position of having to question him, an embarrassing situation for both of us. I wondered how emotionally draining that conversation would be. To my surprise and relief, it was smooth and quick: the second we met, the honorable commander lay his report on the table and said, "The landing checklist was done superficially without verifying that the landing gear was in the correct position. I decided to abort the first landing, and upon my second attempt, everything went normally."

In a short and pointed report, the commander admitted his mistake, pure and simple. He didn't try to blame it on the control tower, even though they had been bombarding him with information, or on the wind and turbulence, which were really strong that day. He did not blame his inexperienced copilot, who was the one who failed to check the landing gear when he told him to. You could clearly hear him giving the order on the CVR.

This man, who was already a hero to me, became even more commendable in that moment through his demonstration of impeccable leadership and humanity, qualities which I rarely see.

Aside from the commander's exemplary professional conduct, that incident also turned out to be incredibly useful because it gave me an idea for a *simulator drill*, which I have put into practice many times over the years. In the drill, I deactivate the "landing-gear-down" command and distract the pilots, playing the role of a talkative control tower, until the pilots verbally confirm "down three green" without actually checking if the landing gear has indeed been lowered.

This man, who was already a hero to me, became even more commendable in that moment through his demonstration of impeccable leadership and humanity, qualities which I rarely see.

By forcing them to come to this incorrect confirmation in the simulator, I train them always to be vigilant. I can guarantee that a good pilot never makes the same mistake twice. In real-life conditions, these pilots never again confirm a procedure before checking to confirm they've executed it, no matter how stressful the situation or how many hundreds of times they have done that procedure in the past.

Considering the commander from the example above, it is quite clear that if anyone has any difficulties comprehending or any knowledge gaps, those are easily solvable with some reading to get to the required level of proficiency. If they have trouble with particular skills or a specific maneuver, they can repeat it as many times as it takes to execute it up to standard.

But how do you turn someone into a leader, a capable commander?

That is the most challenging question to answer, and it is at the center of the entire process of evaluating a copilot seeking to become a commander. The critical ingredient is *responsibility*.

Who Is in Charge?

After the doors close, the engines start, and the plane takes off, the fate of everyone on board is in the hands of the captain. The success of the flight depends on how capable they are of applying all their experience, knowledge, and non-technical ability to make decisions in potential emergencies. Knowing all that, you can imagine how heavy the burden of responsibility is on the evaluation committee. These people decide who gets to make the transition from copilot to captain.

But how do you turn someone into a leader, a capable commander?

Suppose there are harsh conditions, the cockpit is anything but dark, filled with the beeping and pinging of all kinds of alarms. Such situations can escalate quickly because of a significant malfunction. In moments like this, can we rely on any pilot who simply finished their training and ticked all the boxes to handle the situation? How can anyone be a leader without that sense of responsibility? More than once, as an instructor, I found myself in the simulator when an exercise didn't go well or wasn't entirely up to standard, and the commander suddenly blamed their copilot for not helping enough, causing an error that in real life would've probably ended in disaster.

In light of the above, here are three questions that will help you understand how you relate to responsibility.

1. Can You Handle Great Responsibility?

I'll tell it to you straight – some people can't. But the truth is they only think they can't. Here's what we mean: many copilots never even try to take the exams to become a captain because they don't want so much responsibility. They think they wouldn't be able handle it or that it's just not worth the effort. But we all know that anyone, if life pressures them into something, can step up. A mother quickly becomes a lioness if her kid seems to be in danger.

A copilot, if the captain somehow becomes incapacitated, might just step up and handle everything very well. Perhaps another way to ask, "Can you handle great responsibility?" is "Do you really want it and are you ready to pay the price, to bear the pressure?" These are the people who avoid any responsibility – projects, people, assets, decisions. You can't be a leader if you back out of every challenge. What if Michael Jordan had avoided taking any clutch shots? None of us would know him!

You find your opportunity to prove you're a true leader in these crucial moments when no one

- Is rushing to take the three-pointer that wins the basketball game
- Is jumping at the chance to make a big last-minute presentation
- Wants to have a difficult but necessary and urgent conversation with a client

If you shy away from responsibility in crucial moments, you lose face in the eyes of your people faster than a balloon you're trying to inflate loses air the second you let it slip through your fingers. Not a pretty sight, huh?

Responsibility is the price of being the boss.

2. You, Too, Have a Black Box, and It's Even Better Than the One in the Flight Deck. But What Is It Recording?

Your people will see and be influenced by almost everything you do. You might ask yourself: "Must leaders always lead by example?" That question doesn't make much sense if you ask me. Whether they want to or not, leaders are an example for those around them. People keep a close eye on how their leaders react to news, tell the truth, display inappropriate behavior, and report incidents. People remember everything! Some are even able to quote their leaders for years after the fact.

Responsibility is the price of being the boss.

But while planes' black boxes record everything as it happens, dryly and neutrally, people tend to embellish their memories with their interpretations and additions every time they tell the story, depending on their mood, their goals, the rumors they heard, and many other factors. This makes such recountings unpredictable. Two people can have two completely different takes on the way a leader handles the same problem.

What can you do about it? The best thing to do is to assume full responsibility every day, in every situation. Is it a tall order? You betcha. It might even seem impossible, but in reality, it is much better than continually shirking your responsibilities and blaming someone or something else. Who gets blamed? It is the weather, the boss, the clients, the employees, the trainers, the neighbors, or a butterfly in the Amazon Forest flapping its wings, eventually causing a storm at the worst possible moment.

3. And Finally, How Do You See Responsibility?

There are two ways to look at responsibility. One views it as a burden, as something to avoid. The other sees responsibility as an opportunity to grow, meaning the more you take on – more challenging decisions, more significant projects – the more you evolve, making it easier to bring it all to the finish line.

How we view responsibility is our choice. Kids naturally choose the second interpretation. They want to take on responsibilities even when they don't fully understand them or their consequences.

- They want to go to the grocery store alone
- They want to feed their younger brother or sister
- They jump on the ladder to get something from a higher shelf even if that thing weighs more than they do

Sometimes it's funny; other times parents get alarmed. But on the whole, we're glad they want to do things themselves, and we understand that this is how they grow up and mature.

If you're lucky enough to lead a team, that role comes in a package deal with two obligations.

- You can never excuse yourself – you have to take responsibility for your decisions, mistakes, and the consequences of your actions. You have to be able to say, "The buck stops here"– an expression most identified with President Truman, who used the phrase to mean that the final responsibility for his administration's decisions belongs to him, and he would never try to blame it on someone else. The key is to believe it before you say it.

- The second moral obligation is to instill the same sense of responsibility in your team. That is the only way they will evolve and improve.

Don't worry. Once you have the first part locked down, the second one will come much more naturally. Good luck!

Part Three | Control Consistently

7 | Smoke in the Cabin

People often ask me: "What is the worst situation in which pilots can find themselves?"

Many think the answer is engine failure, but that isn't true. If one of the engines gives out mid-flight, we still have the other one (or several), and there is no reason we couldn't complete the journey. All modern airplanes have at least two engines and are certified to fly over vast uninhabited areas like oceans, deserts, and jungles, on a single engine if need be.

Pilots don't just take off and hope for the best – we always have a plan.

If one of the engines suddenly croaks, we're more than capable of landing safely, or even crossing the Atlantic, with the other one. While engine failure is a problem, it's not a big one, and we deal with it with the calm of a pilot. It's one of the scenarios we prepare ourselves for every time we head out to the runway.

Pilots don't just take off and hope for the best – we always have a plan.

What If the Engines Stop?

"But what if the engine is on fire?" Yeah, that one is a little tougher than having one of the engines simply give out. The wings hold the engines. The wings can contain hundreds of tons of fuel. Just to give you an idea, the smallest Airbus can carry around 6,000 gallons of petrol, which is about 18.5 tons. The largest model, the A380, can hold up to 84,500 gallons – that's 256 tons of jet fuel!

Stopping the engine and cutting out its supply of fuel has to be done swiftly. With the help of chemical extinguishers and a healthy flow of air, we can put out the fire immediately, de-escalating the situation to the first scenario described above – a busted engine, in which case, the other engine will bring us to safety.

"But what if the other engine fails, too?" When that question makes an appearance in my classroom, people usually turn around towards the person who asked it and stare, as if to say, "Buddy, whose side are you on here?" They don't actually say it, though, because they are just as curious to hear the answer. Though improbable, a few cases have occurred where all the engines were incapacitated for various reasons: a cloud of volcanic ash, a fuel leak combined with an error in the readings, or flock of geese that destroys both engines. (See the Miracle on the Hudson story in Chapter 5.)

The Power of the Glide

Thankfully, all of the incidents I've mentioned ended well. You might be surprised to learn that modern airplanes will glide. Depending on the altitude at which the engines stop, planes can glide for dozens of miles for more than an hour – just enough time to restart at least one engine or find a place to land.

The longest an airplane has ever glided in history was 120 km (74.5 miles). An Airbus 330 managed to land safely in the Azores after both engines stopped. That gliding ability saved 306 people, and only 2 passengers suffered minor injuries at the evacuation on the runway. Can you imagine? Both engines gave out in the

Atlantic Ocean, and the worst thing that happened was a couple of skinned knees!

Of course, pilots may encounter many different scenarios during their careers, some more complex, others a little easier to handle. That is why manufacturers, test pilots, and airlines are in constant, transparent communication with each other about each incident. We work together to create and implement procedures for every imaginable predicament, each one a new line in the plane triangle we discussed in Chapter 4. Some of these scenarios are absurd and have never happened. Still, pilots train and prepare to handle them.

As I write these lines, I have over 13,000 hours of flight and over 4,500 hours in the simulator, and I have the training to handle special cases. When I train and test other pilots in the simulator, I teach them to deal with any crisis that may come their way. Sometimes I even test would-be flight instructors in flight. When we're in training, up in the air, I simulate a missed approach – it's when, for various reasons, a commander decides to abort a landing and then maneuvers the plane back for another approach – and then I have them land with a single engine.

Smoke in the Cabin and Flight Deck

With all that in mind, the emergency I consider the trickiest and most stressful is smoke in the cabin. It rarely happens, but when it does, the chances of walking away scot-free are unfortunately lower than for the scenarios listed above. It is every pilot's worst nightmare: You're cruising over mountains at 12,000 meters or 39,370 feet, at 900 kph or 560 mph in a 60-ton pressurized metal tube. Other planes are zooming around you, mere miles away. Your 90 kVA generators are powering hundreds of computers, relays, and motherboards on dozens of screens and devices, through thousands of electrical conductors. Now imagine that a fire breaks out somewhere in those 20 km (12.4 miles) of cables and spreads throughout the plane. Soon the cockpit and the passenger cabin are full of smoke, and in a split second, you can't see anything.

How to Prepare for Smoke

Every operation manual for any type of plane, in any airline, extensively addresses this scenario. At least once a year, all pilots go through a dedicated simulator drill, where smoke is released into the mock-cockpit using special smoke generators.

We leave smoke drills for last – they leave you so drained, so devoid of energy, that doing anything else on the simulator afterwards is impossible.

What's the big deal? The plane has oxygen masks, pilots have protective eyewear, and the rest of the plane will continue working normally, at least for a while. Why has smoke in the cabin often ended in tragedy in the past? The problem is that the smoke appears out of the blue and becomes quite dense very quickly. It gets so thick that you can't even tell the time on your wristwatch. You don't see your copilot or the screens – nothing.

Consequently, operating the plane's controls, especially the autopilot, is rendered impossible. In the simulator, crises, however serious, are only mimicked. The pilots know they're not in any real danger and are not responsible for 200 lives on board. Yet, you can literally feel the adrenaline pumping through your veins as your stress rises to a dangerous level.

We leave smoke drills for last – they leave you so drained, so devoid of energy, that doing anything else on the simulator afterwards is impossible.

Emergency!

Let's exercise our minds for a bit: you're the captain; you're at cruising altitude; the passengers are sleeping, reading, talking, or walking around the cabin. You're two hours into the flight, one hour left, and it's been dark cockpit all the way – no CAUTION or WARNING lights whatsoever. Suddenly, you smell something burning, and in two to three seconds, the cockpit is full of smoke. What do we do?

We keep it together, put on our protective masks, and try to identify as quickly as possible where the smoke is coming from, which is in itself an unnerving task. We shut down the plane's systems one by one, trying to figure out which piece of equipment is at fault. Is the smoke coming from the pressurization system or maybe the air-conditioning? While one of the pilots is busy checking and continuously communicating with the cabin crew to learn if the smoke has dissipated, the other pilot flies the plane, as much as the reduced visibility will allow, with the help of air traffic control.

If possible, the plane will descend to lower altitudes. Once it's closer to the ground, the pilots might even open the cockpit window mid-flight to eliminate the smoke. Doing that introduces fresh air and more oxygen into the plane, which might start a fire, but at least the visibility will allow safer maneuvering of the aircraft. Imagine opening the window at 3,000 meters (9,842 feet), going 450 kmh (280 mph).

Nothing about this scenario is routine; everything happens rapidly.

Nothing about this scenario is routine; everything happens rapidly.

As adrenaline kicks in, the pilots are in a state of intense concentration, and the stakes are as high as they can get. Meanwhile, in the passenger cabin, everyone is back in their seats, and you can be sure no one is sleeping, reading, or talking anymore. The oxygen masks are down, and the atmosphere is so strained that you can cut the tension with a knife. The flight attendants are doing what they learned to do with surgical precision, trying to keep things under control through their body language and the tone of their voices, addressing carefully worded commands to the passengers. It is not yet clear how things will turn out.

Let's hit "pause," hover over the cabin, and go over what we need to do.

The only solution here is to have a plan.

As an instructor and commander, I always have a strategy for each of my flights. Prior to stepping inside the cockpit, I always have answers to these questions:

- What do I do if I'm flying over mountains and an engine fails?
- What if they both fail?
- At which airport do I land?
- How far would I need to glide?
- If I make an emergency descent over the mountains, in which direction should I go?
- How far?
- How long?

I make sure I update those plans according to the conditions: the altitude, the landscape, the air traffic, how much fuel I have left, and so on. Even if the odds are stacked against me and smoke starts filling the cabin – I've got it covered.

In the first few moments, when the smoke first infiltrates the cockpit, I only need to set the frequency of the ILS (Instrument Landing System) to a nearby airport. The plane heads here, and the control tower connects to our cockpit. This, however, cannot be done in zero visibility. Or maybe it can, only it would take several precious minutes that can't be spared in an emergency. I'll explain: In the central horizontal console between the pilots, where a car has its transmission, we each have an alphanumeric keyboard and a screen. Altogether, they're 5.8 x 8.3 inches. I have to punch in letters and numbers in a particular sequence, see them on the screen, and confirm. If I manage to punch the code in before I lose visibility, the chances of resolving the situation rise significantly.

After that, we'll have to land the plane blind – we can't see anything through the windows or the screens – which is challenging but doable. If I don't make it to the keyboard in time, everything becomes exponentially more complicated.

The first thing I absolutely must do before anything else is punch that code into that keyboard.

Everything else I can do even if I can't see a thing because I know the cockpit like the back of my hand. I can push all the right buttons and flick all the correct switches to set the plane's altitude and trajectory for landing even without looking. I may not be able to see the data on my screen, but with the help of the air traffic controller, who sees all our coordinates and parameters in real time on their screen in the control tower, I can turn the dials as much as needed to descend, turn, or slow down.

Everything comes down to having a plan and quickly executing it.

Because I know where the handles for the flaps, landing gear, and brakes are, I don't have to see them to operate them, and I can then have the autopilot essentially land the plane for me. You could make a safe landing that way, too.

Everything comes down to having a plan and quickly executing it.

Fire in My Flight Deck

You may be wondering if I've ever had smoke in the cabin on any of my flights.

As luck would have it, the thing you fear most becomes a reality, so yes – I had a case of smoke in the cabin when I flew from Otopeni Airport in Bucharest to Charles de Gaulle in Paris. Here's how that went.

I met the crew in the briefing room an hour before takeoff, as usual. My copilot and I had already gone over the flight details – the weather report, the flight plan, the cargo manifest, etc. – and we were ready to brief the cabin crew. Though the manual spares no detail in describing the preflight briefing, as I'm sure you know from Chapter 5, each commander chooses their way of doing it. It can be an easygoing, friendly atmosphere, where every member of the crew can participate, or a more militaristic, no-frill manner, in which the captain curtly describes the flight plan and assigns everyone's tasks for every emergency.

In my 25 years as an airline pilot, I have learned that when things go south in crisis times, the weakest links usually make the worst mistakes – the least experienced crew members. That is why in every briefing, I carve out time for those who just started in the industry, both to boost their confidence and to make them feel like a part of the team. That fateful flight to Paris was my first time flying with a new hire to our crew, a young flight attendant assigned to the back of the plane. Most of the time, especially in short hauls like Bucharest-Paris, we pilots don't interact much with the flight attendants in the back. We only see them in the briefing room, and after we land back home.

I finished my briefing with a little quiz. I spoke with each member to make sure they knew their part. I asked them to ask me questions if they had any, and then I closed with a joke and left for the plane, smiling. My copilot that day was one of my best friends, who is now a captain. It looked like we were going to have a quiet flight, a perfect dark cockpit.

Everything went according to plan until we reached the Frankfurt area. At 11,500 meters (37,729 feet) and 40 minutes left to the destination, we got a call from the back of the plane. It was the new flight attendant, asking to come into the cockpit. It was very unusual because we usually communicate through the intercom. If there's any critical message that needs to be said in person, the Chief Purser delivers it.

I exchanged looks with my copilot, and after checking the security camera at the entrance to the cockpit, we unlocked the door and let her in. Our young, by now utterly crimson-faced colleague, didn't even know where to start! At last, she mustered up the courage to speak and asked us if we "played around with the lights." Another exchange of looks with my copilot, this time a little annoyed. What did she mean, "played around"?

She explained that a few of the kitchen lights turned on and off a few times, and it wasn't just the lights but the ovens and the coffee machines as well. Then they all turned back on, and that was why she thought we might have had something to do with it.

I was beginning to understand why the Chief Purser didn't come to me herself, preferring to send the new girl into the lion's den in her stead. I assured her that we would never do something like this because we don't treat the plane like a toy, and I thanked her for bringing it to our attention.

Again, we exchanged looks, but we thought nothing of it. We figured some people are just weird, asking bizarre questions. After the young lady left, we looked at the central control and monitoring system, but everything appeared normal.

About ten minutes later, when we had already passed Frankfurt and were preparing to start our descent towards Paris, I looked down to my left to get something out of my briefcase. When I looked up, my worst nightmare was unfolding before me: smoke in the cabin! It was dense, and it had the strong, unmistakable smell of burnt conductor. It only took a second to spread, and it was so thick that I could barely see my copilot, who was sitting a mere three feet away. It was like fog, and it was only getting thicker. It was then that I understood why pilots undergo annual physical checkups and why they have to have healthy hearts – one encounter with smoke in the cabin, and my heart was racing out of my chest.

Mayday, Mayday, Mayday!

Over the years, I've learned to leverage my stress, to make the most out of the adrenaline my body pumps through me in moments like this. Part of this means using the heightened state of awareness and focus that adrenaline provides to execute the plan. The other part of it means having a plan in the first place.

I had a plan for what to do next. I immediately started going over it in my mind. My copilot and I would put on the oxygen masks with the incorporated goggles. We would set the automated landing frequency, reestablish communications, and declare the emergency through the standard call, "Mayday, Mayday, Mayday, this is flight RO 381, smoke in the cockpit, requiring emergency landing

Over the years, I've learned to leverage my stress, to make the most out of the adrenaline my body pumps through me in moments like this. Part of this means using the heightened state of awareness and focus that adrenaline provides to execute the plan. The other part of it means having a plan in the first place.

at Frankfurt. Standby." Next, we'd make an emergency descent towards Frankfurt, now behind us. It took me but a second to make a plan for how we would descend – to the left, where, despite there being mountains, it would go more quickly because there was less traffic under us, whereas on the right, there were eight other planes.

Mayday, Mayday, Mayday is not a message you often hear, so when it does come up on the comms, the control tower and everyone around takes it very seriously and moves very fast. Once they confirm the message, the control tower orders all the other planes to clear the area, which they do without delay because everyone knows exactly how severe the situation is.

Maybe you've seen those maps that show planes in real time – the traffic around airports is so congested that they look like swarms on the map. A Mayday is one way to clear everyone out in less than a minute. With the limited time and space, everyone works in unison, resulting in a veritable spectacle of coordinated air maneuvers. The control tower diverts all airplanes waiting to land so that they go elsewhere to ensure the afflicted plane has the tower's undivided attention and all the room the pilots need.

The air traffic controllers know perfectly well that in critical moments like this, the three things the crew needs most are time, airspace, and quiet.

They do their best to supply all three as they standby for more information from the captain. Meanwhile, on the ground at Frankfurt, the airport's emergency first response teams are called to the scene – technicians, firefighters, EMS, and other personnel. Dozens of vehicles are put into motion in a matter of

The air traffic controllers know perfectly well that in critical moments like this, the three things the crew needs most are time, airspace, and quiet.

minutes, ready to handle anything that may be needed after the plane makes a full stop on the runway.

The same scenario was waiting for us that day, only this time we were going to be at the center of it all. All that was left for us to do was to put on our oxygen masks. But we managed to escape having to land at Frankfurt by the skin of our teeth.

I instantly thought of the young, flushed flight attendant who asked the Chief Purser if the pilots had played around with the kitchen's electricity. I immediately shut off electricity to the passenger cabin, from the plane's front doors to the kitchen in the back. I shut off everything nonessential, leaving only the emergency lighting. It was clear to me, though it didn't show up anywhere in the readings, that one of the electric consumer units had short-circuited.

For several seconds, which felt like an eternity, we waited with our masks on our laps to see if anything I did had any effect. In a few moments, the smoke dissipated as quickly and as abruptly as it had appeared, leaving behind only the smell of burnt fuse. We kept our oxygen masks on our knees until we finally landed in Paris, our original destination, as planned. That was a close call!

When we landed in Paris, the French technicians found a burnt cable from a fan in the air conditioning system in the back of the plane. After they deactivated it, we had the clearance to return to Bucharest without delay.

Though my story of smoke in the cabin had a happy ending, similar deadly scenarios crashed no less than 10 planes in the last 25 years.

What Constitutes Smoke in Your Cabin?

What can you learn from this? How can you handle smoke in your cabin or gain better control of your life? Let me share two pieces of advice: one is more general, the other is specific, but both are equally valuable.

1. All of the Above

You know this expression from multiple-choice questions as the last in a list of possible answers. *All of the above* should be your first takeaway from this chapter. If we think of the previous chapters in this book as possible answers to the question, "How can I stay in control and achieve my goals," the best thing you can do is all of the above.

Striving to excel at everything will significantly increase your chances of succeeding, if not downright guarantee it.

Surely you have goals in life, and *good communication* – the subject of the first part of the book – helps you achieve them. Of course, you want to get the best results out of your people. Your *leadership skills* – the focus of the second part – make all the difference.

Do No Harm

> Striving to excel at everything will significantly increase your chances of succeeding, if not downright guarantee it.

Obviously, you want to do good, but first, you need to make sure you *do no harm*, right? The best way to do that is to apply all the principles that we've discussed so far. Let the title of this segment, *all of the above*, be your first golden rule.

For example, in my smoke-in-the-cabin incident, if I hadn't received the seemingly immaterial scrap of information about the flickering lights in the back of the plane, I would not have had a valuable clue as to where to start controlling the emergency. I would have had to initiate the emergency landing protocol. That has consequences – including the next day's unflattering headline, "Romanian plane forced to make an emergency landing," or its juicier cousin, "Romanian plane in flames over Europe." (At least one journalist is bound to point out that where there's smoke, there's fire).

There would have been additional costs: transferring the passengers from Frankfurt to Paris, grounding the plane, delays, and more. The only reason I knew where to start problem solving was that the young flight attendant who felt comfortable enough to come into the cockpit and talk to me. Undoubtedly, she was one of the key factors that prevented a disaster and saved our lives. Would she have done that if I had kept my distance at the briefing? Probably not.

Recall in Chapter 5, you learned about the importance of every person on the team feeling comfortable to speak up when they are concerned about a safety issue. Every crew member is part of a team focused on having a safe flight. Every person's observations and actions count towards achieving this goal.

Later, when I thought about the incident and tried to retrace my train of thought and why I acted the way I did in those critical moments, I realized that everything significantly contributed to the successful resolution of what was, without a doubt, a potentially catastrophic event:

- My good night's sleep the night before
- How I left home
- My attitude that day
- The way I prepared myself for the flight
- My empathetic and assertive approach at the briefing that made our newest member feel confident in speaking up

None of it was by accident. You can never chalk everything up to "dumb luck," can you? For the most part, "dumb luck" results from preparation, many little actions done the right way, at the right time.

After we close the door to the plane and take off towards our destination, it is up to us to solve problems as they appear, and we can only do that if we work together.

I do not consider a single member of my crew redundant. We must make it to our destination safely, day in and day out, mission after mission, rain, ice, lightning, turbulence, or shine, every single time.

After we close the door to the plane and take off towards our destination, it is up to us to solve problems as they appear, and we can only do that if we work together.

In certain situations, you are the sum of the actions and the decisions that have led you to that point. When a sports team wins the championship, not only the season's victories or the luck of the draw got them there, but also:

- The losses
- The lessons learned
- The teammates' discipline
- The years of practice and dedication
- Their individual characters
- The dynamics between them
- Their leadership

These are all things that pave their way to the top.

2. What If?

How did I make it out of the smoke in the cabin incident? I had a plan. In aviation, we have a plan for everything. Do you?

What if? is a question you should be asking yourself before you start doing anything.

- What if something comes up?
- What will you do?
- And what if things don't go according to plan?
- What are you going to do then?

The higher the stakes, the more critical it is to ask yourself those "What if?" questions. How you complete them is up to you. In the beginning, you'll probably have to draw on your imagination, though for many people, that usually consists of coming up with one exceedingly optimistic scenario after another. Maybe you have a big presentation at work, and your "what if" is, "What if the client stops me ten seconds into the presentation and tells me 'stop right there, you had us at hello with your can-do attitude, where do we sign?'"

What if? is a question you should be asking yourself before you start doing anything.

That scenario doesn't warrant any special preparation because the probability of that happening is close to zero, and the only plan you need to make is how and where to celebrate.

But how do you know which "what ifs" you should be asking yourself? In your day-to-day life, your primary way of knowing is one that often comes at a steep price – *personal experience.* The more experienced you are, the more "what ifs" you have because you will know what to expect, how to respond to the unexpected, and how not to repeat your mistakes.

That is why I always say, if you have a deficit in experience, it is best to learn from someone else's experience: from books and manuals, from conversations you have with others, or even from observation, taking a mental note of what works and what could be done better.

After all, it hurts a lot less to learn from other pilots'

emergencies than to go through them yourself. That is the primary reason pilots go through retraining in simulators after a plane emergency that took place somewhere else in the world.

Take sporting competitions, for example, where many things can turn out completely different than what you expect. Without anticipating worst case scenarios and preparing for them, there's no way you're going to beat a skilled opponent. Or take a more familiar example: When you have a presentation to make, you can and should prepare for a long list of what-ifs. Your ability to quickly adapt to different situations will affect your success a lot more than the font you chose for your slides or even their actual content.

> That is why I always say, if you have a deficit in experience, it is best to learn from someone else's experience: from books and manuals, from conversations you have with others, or even from observation, taking a mental note of what works and what could be done better.

In aviation, the successful resolution of crises has less to do with a pilot's skills or cunning and a lot more to do with their attitude in an emergency, with their discipline and rigorous execution of standard procedures. Still, most importantly, it has to do with their ability to plan for every imaginable outcome, every contingency. On a busy day, up to 30,000 planes soar through the air worldwide, and it is the combination of knowledge, skills, and the right attitude that makes this synchronized dance between them possible, and above all – safe.

How many of us secretly hope, upon occasion, that everything will be fine: that things will fall into place, or that problems will miraculously resolve themselves? Sometimes that is exactly what happens! We don't do anything, or we freeze, and we don't know how to react or what to do, but somehow, we manage to walk away intact from a potentially dangerous situation.

Some people may take it as a sign that you can leave it up to fate and that everything will be OK. But how often do miracles happen? How often does a problem that negatively impacts a company, an organization, a group of people, or a single person – or even an entire country – get magicked away?

Imagine pilots who are about to fly through a storm. Instead of thinking of where to land in case of emergency along the way or getting extra fuel for a detour, they cross their fingers and hope things work out. Would you get on that flight?

The late author Peter F. Drucker, whose work laid many of the foundations for modern business practices, used to say, "Miracles are great, but they're so unpredictable."

He was right: you can't (nor should you) depend on a miracle to do your job for you, and you certainly can't count on its punctuality.

What can you do to make sure you're always in control? Whenever you prepare to do something, anything, ask yourself as many what-ifs as you can conjure to make sure you're covered if things go sideways. Prepare yourself for those worst-case scenarios and the scenarios that may not be that bad but are very likely. Be ready to get out of the situation on top. For the unlikely "medium-case" scenarios, I suggest you at least have a plan prepared in your mind, just in case.

The late author Peter F. Drucker, whose work laid many of the foundations for modern business practices, used to say, "Miracles are great, but they're so unpredictable."

What if is one of man's best friends, right up there with dogs and trash cans (and of course, their electronic version – the Delete button). Big corporations don't cough up a single cent until they have market surveys, analysis, and alternative plans.

Why would it be any different for individuals? Get friendly with your what-ifs.

Why is it essential to have a plan for every eventuality? The answer is simple: you can make the most out of life, keep your stress levels to a minimum, and optimize your chances of achieving everything you want.

8 | 50 Causes of an Accident

The darkest day in aviation history was March 27th, 1977, when two Boeing 747 Jumbo Jets, one operated by KLM, the other by Pan Am, collided on Tenerife Airport's runway, resulting in the death of 583 people. (Tenerife is one of the Canary Islands off Spain.)

Why would we dig into this painful tragedy and stir so many unpleasant emotions by picking at the gruesome details? We do it because we owe it to those who are no longer with us to learn something from this disaster.

Let's look into it together.

The Site of the Collision

The Canary Islands have always been a top tourist destination, attracting millions of visitors from all over the world every year. Most of them come to the Canary Islands by plane, so the archipelago's three airports, Gran Canaria, Tenerife, and Lanzarote, can get quite crowded around high season.

Why would we dig into this painful tragedy and stir so many unpleasant emotions by picking at the gruesome details? We do it because we owe it to those who are no longer with us to learn something from this disaster.

If you go on vacation in the Canary Islands at peak season and happen to stay close to an airport, you'll see planes taking off and landing almost constantly, sometimes as often as every 60 seconds. If you look up, you'll see at least four, five, six planes neatly lined up, waiting to get the tower's OK to land.

It wasn't as crowded in the Canaries in the 1970s as it is now, but tourists were still coming and going all the time. On that fateful day, March 27th, 1977, the main airport on the islands, Las Palmas in Gran Canaria, was shut down due to a bombing, for which a group of political extremists claimed responsibility. Naturally, air traffic control immediately redirected all the flights that were supposed to land at Las Palmas to Tenerife North Airport, the only airport on the island back then – small, quiet, and with not nearly enough space and personnel for the massive volume of incoming flights.

Where Do We Put All the Planes?

The airport quickly reached its full capacity. In less than two hours, the two parking areas ran out of room, as this was the first time the small airport had ever had to serve so many planes at once. The control tower's load quickly grew out of hand, demanding the controllers' undivided attention, which was already pushed to the limit. The ground handling crews were overwhelmed as well, and the ramps, tractors, fuel tanks, and other machinery proved insufficient for the sheer volume of arrivals, causing many delays.

Since the airport was almost completely full, the planes started parking on the airport's only taxiway, which ran parallel to the runway, forcing the planes that were preparing for takeoff to taxi on the runway to the other end and make a U-turn (backtrack) to reposition themselves for takeoff. All of this took four or five times longer than what it would usually take to get a plane off the ground, which in turn caused more and more delays and added to everyone's already burgeoning stress levels.

Delays, Delays and More Delays

Some of the planes landing at Tenerife North were coming in after a long trip, almost entirely out of fuel, so they had to refuel at the airport to continue on their journey. Every pilot on the premises knew that this detour from the destination airport would mean more delays that would ripple out to the rest of the airline's activity. Every additional delay increased the probability that the return flight would be canceled because the crew would exceed its legal amount of work hours.

On top of that, the weather wasn't cooperative. Visibility was terrible due to thick fog covering large portions of the runway and taxiway, blocking the control tower's view of the moving aircraft.

Visibility Drops

On top of that, the weather wasn't cooperative. Visibility was terrible due to thick fog covering large portions of the runway and taxiway, blocking the control tower's view of the moving aircraft.

As if that wasn't enough, it was getting dark, making it even more difficult for the controllers and the pilots to see anything.

Stress Mounts

Everyone was on edge. The planes were maneuvered slowly and carefully, and the delays were piling up. Crowds of increasingly irritated tourists filled the terminal. Their current predicament was the furthest thing away from how they had imagined they would spend their vacation.

After a few hours of this, the Gran Canaria airport reopened, and the planes that were originally supposed to land there started getting ready for takeoff. All the captains decided to take extra fuel to prevent any further delays, with the intent of dropping off the incoming passengers at their initial destination and then immediately taking off with the outbound passengers.

Getting Ready for Take Off

Let's zoom in on the scene of the accident. The American Pan Am Boeing 747 was ready to take off. It had refueled, and all passengers were on board, but a Dutch KLM Boeing 747 and a fuel tank blocked the runway's access. The two Jumbo Jets' wingspan didn't allow for the two planes to pass each other safely on the narrow taxiway. The entire length of the other side of the taxiway, parallel to the runway, was occupied by other planes. Therefore, the Pan Am plane had to wait another 35 minutes for the KLM plane to finish refueling.

When they finally finished, the KLM plane started boarding, which in itself caused more delays because, as it sometimes happens, a few of the passengers – a Dutch family – were late getting to the gate on time. Another passenger decided to stay in Tenerife. She was the sole survivor on the KLM passenger list that day.

The refueling, the boarding, finding the missing passengers, and the formalities of processing the passenger's cancellation added more than an hour of wait time.

You can imagine the tension in each flight deck and the control tower, and how annoyed all the passengers were because of all the delays. That's two Jumbo Jets full of ticked-off people!

Eventually, the control tower directed the two planes to go one after the other in the same direction on the airport's only runway. The KLM plane was first. It was supposed to go to the other end of the runway, where it would backtrack and wait for permission to take off. The air traffic controller told the Pan Am crew to taxi to the third exit off the runway towards the taxiway, where it could clear the way for the KLM plane to take off.

You can imagine the tension in each flight deck and the control tower, and how annoyed all the passengers were because of all the delays. That's two Jumbo Jets full of ticked-off people!

It Gets Worse

Although things weren't great up until that point – delays, overcrowding, and high-stress levels – they were still manageable. But from that moment on, they took an even worse turn. Because of the fog, the Pan Am crew couldn't see the third exit and continued to the end of the runway. They could have turned on the fourth exit, which would have been even better for them because it was at a 30° angle and not 120° like the exit they had missed, but the poor visibility left them unsure of their whereabouts.

We Are Cleared for Takeoff – or Are We?

Meanwhile, the KLM crew did not inform the control tower that they had reached the other end of the runway. To make things worse, the Dutch captain misunderstood the control tower's transmission. He believed he was cleared to take off once he was in position.

Even though the copilot and the onboard engineer weren't sure that the plane was indeed granted permission to take off, and the engineer even tried to warn him, the commander went ahead. He began roaring the engines to full speed and set the plane hurtling down the runway, where the Pan Am pilot was still trying to figure out which turn to take.

The Dutch commander ignored his colleagues and proceeded with the takeoff, shutting each of them down.

The control tower asked the Pan Am pilot to inform them when they cleared the runway, but the transmission was disrupted, and none of the pilots fully received it. But that was enough to rouse the Dutch engineer's suspicions regarding the Pan Am plane's position, suspicions that he communicated to his captain.

The Dutch commander ignored his colleagues and proceeded with the takeoff, shutting each of them down.

Forty tons heavier due to the extra fuel it had taken on to avoid further delays at Gran Canaria, the plane now needed more time and a greater distance to gain enough speed to detach from the ground.

The American crew suddenly saw the Dutch plane's takeoff lights speeding towards them, and although they couldn't believe what they were seeing, they immediately reacted and tried to turn their aircraft onto the lawn on the left at full speed. The Dutchmen suddenly saw the other plane and tried to leap over the American aircraft. They almost made it, too, with half the plane and the front landing gear barely passing over Pan Am. Unfortunately, they were still too slow to fully take off, resulting in a terrible collision, the KLM Jumbo Jet hitting the Pan Am Boeing at 160 miles per hour right over the wings, crushing the back of the plane, and instantly killing 335 of the American airline's passengers.

After that, the rest of the KLM plane violently rotated for another tenth of a mile, causing a massive explosion and a fire that could not be put out for hours after the collision, ending the lives of all 248 people on board.

Miraculously, 61 people who happened to be in the front of the American plane survived the crash, but they had to jump out of the burning plane by themselves because no one even came to their rescue. The fog was so thick that the emergency first response teams thought that only the KLM plane had crashed; they couldn't see the flaming Pan Am plane in the middle of the runway.

Inside the Cockpit

I obtained the audio recordings of the communication between the two planes and the control tower from that horrible accident, chronologically arranged, including the conversations in each cockpit. Every time I listened to it, I got shivers down my spine. I recognized every element. I entirely understood the strained atmosphere in each cockpit, the crew's exasperation with the delays, the slight rivalry between the two airlines, and the control tower's frustration with the fog obstructing their view of the runway.

You can hear the exact communication on those recordings, the explicit messages, and their confirmations by the control tower or one of the pilots. Still, it was full of interference, and none of the parties seemed to realize that their messages were *neither transmitted nor received.*

Causes of the Crash

The KLM captain, Van Zanten, was one of the most experienced in the company, a respected flight instructor with quite a bit of pull at the airline. Van Zanten was one of the three pilots who had gone to Seattle in 1971 to fly KLM's first Boeing 747 back to its new home base. He was such a big deal that before it was known in Amsterdam that he was the captain at the accident in Tenerife, the airline assigned him to investigate it!

The investigation of the crash listed almost 50 causes, including a series of little oversights and coincidences.

The day of the crash was Commander Van Zanten's first time flying in 12 weeks, which could explain his slight inadequacy on that particular flight. His "iron fist" manner of running things, where no one dared question his decisions, was also an explanation for why his copilots were hesitant to voice their doubts about whether the control tower had permitted them to take off.

The investigation of the crash listed almost 50 causes, including a series of little oversights and coincidences.

There were many additional factors that led to the devastating accident. Some were major, like the reduced visibility and the radio interferences. In contrast, the analysis considered others merely "contributing" factors, like the use of nonstandard phraseology and the unusually high volume of traffic at the airport.

For example, the investigators discovered that while the control tower transmitted communications and directed the traffic, there was a soccer match playing in the background, which might have partially distracted the controllers.

The decision to supplement the plane's fuel reserve with an extra 40 tons increased the distance and speed the aircraft needed to get off the ground and amplified the explosion. However, that seemed to be the correct decision under those circumstances.

A few weeks before the accident, KLM had introduced new strict regulations regarding the restrictions on the crew's work, flight, and rest hours, which may have put pressure on the crew to hurry up and take off so as not to exceed them.

The third exit where the control tower instructed the American pilots to enter the taxiway was at an odd angle, which might have contributed to the crew's confusion as to their exact position.

An unfortunate overlap of legislation loopholes, faulty training, and many banal mistakes coinciding with bad luck led to the biggest accident in aviation history!

I say "banal" mistakes because I can't think of a single flight that didn't share at least some characteristics and thought patterns with the Tenerife disaster.

Legislation has since changed dramatically, and Crew Resource Management (Chapter 5) with which you're already familiar is now an integral part of the aviation industry. As for the banal mistakes and coincidences, there have been significant improvements in reducing and preventing them, but we're still working on that.

Sources of Pressure

One problem is that both the airlines and passengers put pilots under unbelievable pressure never to exceed their work hours and always be on time. Passengers are rarely familiar with or empathetic as to what causes a delay – be it bad weather enroute or at the destination, or because another plane blocks the runway. Passengers constantly demand explanations from the Chief Purser. Consequently, the Chief Purser passes on the passengers' exasperation to the cockpit, where the two pilots are already annoyed with their competitors from the plane that's blocking the runway. The pilots have to delay takeoff further because a few passengers got lost in the airport's duty-free shops.

The Improvements that Occurred After the Collision

Despite all the sources of pressure, an accident like the one in Tenerife could never happen today. This accident instigated a fundamental change in how pilots communicate with each other and with the control tower. It was the springboard for incorporating Crew Resource Management concepts in the aviation industry, making it an integral part of the work dynamics in airlines worldwide. These changes resulted from the accident investigations conducted by hundreds of professionals, representatives of aeronautical authorities in Spain, the Netherlands, and the United States, collaborating with both airlines, and the aircraft manufacturer, Boeing.

First, all radio communication has been standardized. For example, the phrase "take off" can never be used outside the context of the plane getting permission to leave the ground or the confirmation of that permission.

We have radio interferences today as well – there is not a single flight where you wouldn't have similar interferences caused by simultaneous transmissions on the same frequency. It happens every day: The ATC (Air Traffic Control) orders you to switch to another frequency, you change the channel, listen for a second to make sure no other plane or air controller is talking, and you transmit your message, informing them of your position and altitude.

At the same moment you transmit your message, another plane transmits theirs, and the two messages overlap without any of the speakers made aware. The significant difference nowadays, as opposed to Tenerife, is that you may no longer end a radio communication without confirmation of the message. If there's any doubt that a message has been understood correctly, everyone repeats it. This shows that a radio communication is not like a phone conversation, where each message is usually said once. In radio communication, if there is any doubt about the message, it might be said up to four times. If you hadn't read about Tenerife, you would have thought it crazy to keep repeating messages over and over again, wouldn't you? It doesn't seem so silly now, does it?

The cockpit hierarchy is largely the same as it was in the 70's – the commander has the final say on how to conduct the flight, but the concepts of CRM prevent them from making all the decisions alone. A copilot may be a complete beginner, but by definition, their role is *much more significant* now; they are a part of the decision-making process. Now we teach our copilots to ask for explanations from their commanders when something is unclear. On the other hand, no matter how experienced the commander is, we instruct them to listen to the copilot's safety concerns, and they're obligated to take them into consideration.

The Challenging Environment

In its unique way, commercial aviation is a problematic industry, as it operates in what many consider a hostile environment:

- Meteorological phenomena like wind and rain
- Reduced visibility at takeoff and landing
- Obstructions and problematic braking conditions on the runway
- The landscape around an airport

Mix in the human factors, such as

- Extensive and lengthy process of training pilots, flight attendants, and technicians
- Fatigue
- Constant pressure to keep up with the public's demand for punctuality
- Aircraft upkeep

These factors create an intricate picture of all the things an airline must keep track of when operating flights, as well as all the things that can go wrong.

For each risk or component we've listed above, airlines employ *protective operation restrictions* – means by which the airline minimizes or, if possible, completely eliminates those dangers. For example, an airline might forbid certain maneuvers or cancel a flight in problematic weather like strong winds at takeoff or landing, reduced visibility, or the crew exceeding the legal limit of working hours.

Of course, the only way to entirely prevent aviation accidents is not to fly at all – keep the plane grounded and only allow passengers to visit it without taking off. But even in such constrained conditions, you wouldn't be able to avoid all risks – there's bound to be a passenger who falls down because they were looking at their phone instead of where they were going or someone who leans in a little too hard on the open cockpit window. Besides, doing that would completely defeat commercial aviation's purpose, which is to transport people and goods.

Aeronautics accounted for roughly 15% of the world economy, both directly and indirectly in pre-pandemic times. Coping with the Covid pandemic and its impact on travel made us aware of how our lives were built around the ability to easily travel without thinking we were risking infection by walking into a plane. The pandemic added another layer of sanitizing practices to minimize the spread of Covid.

Regulations and More Regulations

Everything in aviation is regulated. The plane's complex systems are built and tested for reliability, so they work well not only on their own but also in constant interaction and coordination with other components.

In the plane's CRS (Certificate of Release to Service) and LE (Loose Equipment), next to the list of things that comprise the aircraft and its systems, there is also a list of all onboard emergency equipment: from lifeboats, fire extinguishers, and axes to megaphones and portable oxygen masks. Adding or removing anything from that list necessitates a careful study of its impact on the aircraft's operation and the release of a new Certificate of Airworthiness.

These documents go into extreme detail, and to someone from the outside, some of the requirements may seem ridiculous. Back in my AN24 piloting days, many of my colleagues complained about not having anywhere to hang their coats in the cockpit. Behind the commander's chair was a metallic shelf on which there was some radio equipment and other electronic components. The shelf was aluminum, and under it, you could have easily added a hook or two for hanging your coat. To this day, I remember how surprised we all were when we learned how daunting the procedure was for getting that small hook installed: the forms, the approvals, the ridiculous cost. So, when we say "protective" restrictions, the term is not just for show.

Layers of Protection

No amount of protection is 100% foolproof, however thoroughly thought out.

After an accident, we can always find a design flaw or faults in something that seems perfect on paper but does not hold up in more complex real-life usage. This flaw reveals its limits and weaknesses. What can we do, then? The obvious and most common solution in the industry, especially after the Tenerife accident – which only highlighted a need for stricter safety standards – is to plan and implement multiple protection layers. The purpose of this redundancy is to make sure that even if one (or more than one) of those layers isn't perfect, you can still rely on the others to pick up the slack.

That's what we do in aviation, and that should be your approach, too – do everything in your power to stay on top of the situation. This guidance applies to your place of work as well as your home life.

No amount of protection is 100% foolproof, however thoroughly thought out.

Swiss Cheese Model of Accident Causation

Whenever an incident or, in worse cases, an accident, happens in aviation, whether or not there were victims involved, a mixed team of experienced pilots, engineers, mechanics, and psychologists conduct a thorough investigation to get down to the bottom of it. Their report provides a detailed overview of how and why the metaphorical Swiss cheese holes overlapped on that particular flight.

The accident in Tenerife is the most tragic real-life example of the Swiss Cheese Model. Let me pose another "Buddy, whose side are you on?" type of question. What if all of your protection layers have faults, "holes," and they happen to overlap and leave you vulnerable?

This concept is called the Swiss Cheese Model of Accident Causation, developed in 1990 by James Reason, a British psychologist. Imagine several slices of Swiss cheese, all with holes, some bigger, some smaller, in different places. Usually, if you lined up a few random slices like domino pieces, you wouldn't be able to see through the holes because they wouldn't overlap. Well, when accidents happen, it is exactly because the unimaginable occurs, and those holes do overlap so that you can see from one end of the Swiss cheese domino trail to the other.

In aviation, medicine, construction, and maybe a few other professions, those mistakes can cost something you can't put a price on – human lives.

The image I have in my head when I think about that terrible accident is that of an arrow breezing through several layers of protection, all generally robust and solid, except for their small holes, which are just wide enough for the arrow to fly through unhindered when they happen to overlap.

When the holes overlap in other professions – IT, banking, and so on – the price of mistakes is money, delays, or lost clients.

In aviation, medicine, construction, and maybe a few other professions, those mistakes can cost something you can't put a price on – human lives.

Minimizing Risks: Getting Ready for Work

There are many possible risks on any flight or any other endeavor people undertake. How can we take control and not leave it all up to fate?

Let me tell you about my strategy, which I consciously employ on every mission to ensure flight safety, no matter what happens. Firstly, I am very aware of the way I prepare myself for work. I channel my inner aviation-accident-investigator and try to find the little things that might later be considered small, strange coincidences, and I eliminate them. Remember the story in Chapter 7 of the lights that went off and on? A coincidence or a warning?

It's like the opening credits of *Fort Apache, The Bronx*. For the first few minutes, all you see on the screen is the torso of a man – a cop, you soon find out – who's getting ready for work. You see him gearing up, one piece of equipment or clothing at a time. The whole scene lasts for quite a while, clearly an artistic stunt by the director. It was fascinating to watch how Paul Newman's character methodically transformed himself from an ordinary man, a civilian, to an exemplary police officer, uniform and all.

I've always thought of myself as a person who builds up his state of mind before going to work the same way someone might build a brick house or an intricate mosaic floor – piece by piece, leveling and reinforcing it, creating a strong base that can withstand whatever one throws at it. That's what I do – I mentally prepare for the day ahead. I pay attention to every detail, and I leave my house in a perfect uniform (figuratively and literally, in my case), putting my best foot forward.

On the way to the airport, I could find countless reasons to get annoyed while I'm in traffic. I could allow myself irritation at the speedsters on the highway, some of whom zigzag across the road with no warning and no respect for the rules or anyone else's safety, forcing me to brake to let them in the lane in front of me.

Come to Work Relaxed

Some years ago, the road to Otopeni Airport was almost always jammed because of simultaneous construction work on several bridges. What would generally be a ten-minute drive was now nearly an hour long. We all used to come to the airport already on edge, and it was enough to have a single person – a ground agent, a mechanic, or who knows who else – to make a single mistake for us to blow up. And that's long before takeoff!

I quickly realized what was happening, and with Tenerife 1977 in mind, I started spending my hour in traffic listening to classical music, breezing over every bump on the road. I would get to work so relaxed that my coworkers would ask me how I managed to keep my cool. I would always answer that we hadn't even taken off yet, and we had a three-, four-, or even thirteen-hour mission ahead of us.

How could I let trivial things like traffic ruin my day before it even began?

Quickly Resolve Problems

The second part of my strategy is to resolve and immediately communicate any elements or details that might cause a problem, even if I could theoretically put them off for later. In Chapter 1, I explained what a dark cockpit was, and I also told you about CAUTION lights (which signal defects that don't require immediate attention but have to be kept in mind) and WARNING lights (which signal defects that require you to act immediately). A CAUTION light usually signals a minor defect that doesn't have a significant or immediate impact on the flight's safety.

How could I let trivial things like traffic ruin my day before it even began?

Despite that, I always teach my future pilots never to put off fixing a problem if they can help it.

Don't let a minor issue become a vulnerability or a stroke of bad luck. In addition, a minor defect might coincide with another defect or a severe CAT (Clear Air Turbulence) and a disconnected autopilot or a sudden deceleration or acceleration. These mundane occurrences require quite a bit of the pilot's attention span, leading to a much bigger problem, having to deal with multiple issues all at once. Besides, what if anything else went wrong? What if the holes start to overlap? The small details start to add up.

> Despite that, I always teach my future pilots never to put off fixing a problem if they can help it.

Visual Approach

We pilots have an exercise we like to repeat in every simulator session: *Visual Approach*. It means landing at an airport with almost no automation: no autopilot, no FD (Flight Director), sometimes even with no A/THR – autothrust, which controls the engine power. When you work for an airline, it could be years before you get a chance to make an unassisted landing in real life. It's not usually approved, even if both pilots are in agreement.

Even though the pilots may want the practice, some airlines never approve such landing procedures, despite the costs it can save the company, both in time and fuel. They train their pilots to do them only on the FFS (Full Flight Simulator). The airline's position is that they have already invested hundreds of millions of dollars in a modern, state-of-the-art plane and so prefer their pilots to use all the automatic features their investment has to offer.

I prefer a pilot who uses all those fancy features and gadgets to get a better overview of the plane at different stages of the flight but who can still keep their cool when manually operating the plane in any situation, even a stressful one. But you can't do that without hands-on experience outside the simulator.

Pilots who never learn to employ the plane's auto-features correctly don't understand the autopilot's role and how to use it properly. As a result, they have caused too many accidents, especially with the plane's airspeed and the rapid succession of events quickly escalating the situation and causing confusion.

In those situations, the appropriate level of automation would be to disconnect the autopilot, the FD, and the autothrust and to fly the plane manually while keeping it at the right speed and position – your basic *skills, pitch, & thrust.*

There is an order to a Visual Approach, a set of milestones and their respective time marks that one must meet before the plane starts descending towards the runway. The pilot who does not meet them must initiate a *Go Around* procedure – the *missed approach* I mentioned earlier.

Pilots who never learn to employ the plane's auto-features correctly don't understand the autopilot's role and how to use it properly. As a result, they have caused too many accidents, especially with the plane's airspeed and the rapid succession of events quickly escalating the situation and causing confusion.

A manual approach is much quicker than landing with the autopilot. That approach requires the pilot to anticipate the next moves. The most common mistake I see beginners make in this exercise is putting off making all the subtle maneuvers that allow the landing's correct configuration.

Picture powerlifters who can lift 440 pounds, but only if they do it right. They find their feet's exact position; they grip the bar just right; they coordinate their entire body to lift the weight and achieve that gold-winning posture. But if they just swung the weight over their head and tried to figure it out as they went, chances are they'd injure their back!

What Superior Pilots Do

Make all preparations in advance. Some pilots have "the touch," as we say, a knack for handling the plane. They can make a perfect landing even if they

- Disconnect all the automated functions at once
- Set all the parameters
- Turn in descent
- Account for the wind
- Reset and turn on the timer to know how much they need to pull up from the runway
- Configure the flaps and the landing gear, accounting for the correct speeds
- Make the PA landing announcement
- Many other little things that have to be done before landing

That is too long a sequence to leave for the last possible second.

At the risk of annoying you – as it annoys some of them – this is exactly the type of pilot to whom I recommend paying more attention and planning their maneuvers in advance, one at a time. I do that so they don't risk breaking their backs like the powerlifter, trying to show off or rely too much on their natural gift.

I remind them of Tenerife, March 27th, 1977, and those 50 causes behind an accident, but also that in my 26 years of flying, too often I've heard of accidents involving "the best pilot in the fleet."

Do you know what "the best pilot in the fleet" means? I'll let you in on another trade secret that I learned years ago and that often pops up in my mind. It goes like this:

"Superior pilots use their superior knowledge to avoid a situation where they have to use their superior skills."

The real trick is not how to get out of trouble, but how to avoid it altogether.

Thus, we conclude my lessons from the Tenerife tragedy and how I apply them every day. What can you learn from this that would help you be more in control of your life? Here are a few suggestions.

> "Superior pilots use their superior knowledge to avoid a situation where they have to use their superior skills."

1. Look Beyond the Leading Causes

After a few heated debates, KLM assumed responsibility for the accident, acknowledging that the plane should never have initiated takeoff without clear-cut confirmation from the control tower. They paid fines and restitution to the victims' families and significantly adjusted their procedures to ensure that nothing like this ever happens again.

When failures occur, many companies and organizations quickly identify and deal with the *primary* cause. I'm not telling you anything new here. Organizations that excel in their field go deeper in their investigations, discussing, analyzing, and taking steps to make sure that the same mistake does not repeat itself. But how many companies do you know make the effort of looking for 20, 30, or 40 things that went wrong and played a part in a significant incident? I would say not many, if any.

The main reason for conducting an extensive investigation shouldn't be to point fingers and punish the guilty party but to understand what happened and learn from it so that you can take not just some but all possible preventive measures in the future. Even when you think you got to the bottom of a problem, it's better to inquire some more and try to find more possible causes. You should only stop when you hear yourself saying, "We wouldn't be in this mess if it weren't for Moses parting the Red Sea" – I mean, there's no use going back to "and if Eve had only left that fruit alone." I'm joking, of course, but my point is that you have to dig deep.

Quality control and quality assurance fields offer tools for deep investigations such as root cause analysis, fishbone diagrams, the 5 Whys Method and Six Sigma techniques. They encourage you to go beyond the first explanation of an incident.

Start your day on the right foot and quickly bounce back from any mishaps because frequently that's when you hit another snag, and a little problem suddenly becomes a big one. Take, for example, a car accident where a vehicle hits a pedestrian at a crosswalk. It may be evident that neither the driver nor the pedestrian was paying attention at the time of the accident. Still, in many cases, their absentmindedness did not just begin a few seconds before the impact, but a few good hours before it, starting with a piece of bad news or a botched job, an unfriendly glare, a nasty rumor, or maybe a few misspoken words. Or perhaps it was the weather.

2. You Can't Be in Control If You Don't Take Control

> Sometimes, someone might be at fault, but to attribute our successes and failures to someone else is as good as declaring that we have no control and we're at the mercy of the elements.

If there's one thing you can always do in life, it is find someone to blame. Whether out loud or merely in our heads, we've all been guilty of this. Every single person involved in the accident at Tenerife could have blamed someone or something else for what had happened.

- The air traffic controllers could have blamed the weather – a "recurring role" in many stories about aviation accidents

- KLM could have blamed the airport's faulty radio equipment and the busy frequency
- Pan Am could have taken a swing at the incompetence of the air traffic controllers
- The passengers could have chalked it up to the terrorists who bombed Gran Canaria

We can always find someone to blame, both to make us feel better and to keep up appearances.

Sometimes, someone might be at fault, but to attribute our successes and failures to someone else is as good as declaring that we have no control and we're at the mercy of the elements.

You might be thinking, "Well, obviously they're not solely responsible, but we can't ignore them, can we? Didn't you just tell us to leave poor Eve out of it?" And you'd be right. I did say that because we can rarely influence what others do. However, to stay on top of the situation, we can mind how *we* behave and set goals that have to do with us, not the weather or other people.

At the end of a game, we might say, "The other team beat us," or we might go with, "We didn't have the necessary physical, psychological, technical, and tactical ability to beat them. We have our work cut out for us, but we can do it." Do you see the difference?

This is exactly why you should always take care of your CAUTION lights as soon as possible – you never know for sure what the future holds, but you sure can be prepared for it. Why hand in your projects before the deadline? You don't know what might happen the morning you planned to finish the job, but you can show up that morning with your project already complete.

If you blame others, you're a victim. Is that really what you want to be? I doubt that. To be in control, you need to do and think about a lot, but it's worth it. It means having the peace of mind of a job well done, not to mention feeling like a functional member of society – a hero! – instead of a helpless burden on those around.

3. Don't Be a Show-off

Speaking of heroes, here's a caveat to my previous point. No one likes a braggart, regardless of how proficient that person is at what they do. Most of the time, they turn out to be full of hot air, anyway. You've probably met people who are so full of it that when someone asks them to prove their skills, they come up empty. It's hilarious when it happens to someone else, but it's not so funny anymore when your team's reputation is on the line, and you can't deliver because somebody got cocky.

It's like those soccer players who pull out all the stops in showpiece matches, balancing the ball on their head or bouncing it off different body parts. Billiard players make cool geometric patterns with the white ball. Tennis players make a shot in between the other player's legs. You never see them doing it in an actual game, do you? In a real match, they keep it neat, they concentrate, and you rarely see any fancy trickery – only as a last resort or when they're no longer worried about winning.

4. Where Do You Draw the Line?

To prevent accidents in aviation, we have conditions under which we decide not to fly, some of which we described earlier. Do you, your team, your company, or even your family have the same? Do you know when to back out? How clear are the conditions in which it is better to avoid working with someone, delivering a product, taking a meeting, or rescheduling?

In some trades, especially the food industry, there are clear quality standards, and when a business fails to meet them, it may be fined or even shut down. How clear are your team's standards for quality? Some companies have a lovely list of company values, neatly presented, and ignored entirely. They exist mainly as an idealistic picture rather than actual guidelines for proper conduct and etiquette or criteria for hiring, firing, and rewarding an employee. It's hard to be in control when you have no clear idea of how being in control looks. How do you define your team spirit, if not as a shared commitment to do certain things at a certain level?

5. 50 for the Good, 50 for the Bad

Consider this: If there are 50 causes of an accident, there must be 50 good factors involved in a success. If an accident can be caused by dozens of contributing factors, from "strange coincidences" to its leading causes, doesn't it stand to reason that success has just as many driving forces behind it?

That is what parents have been telling their children for generations – don't cut corners, don't slack off, be thorough, and do your best because you will never achieve true success through coincidences and shortcuts.

It confirms what the most successful hotels and restaurants around the world always tell you – that every little detail counts, and it is with that principle in mind that they train their chefs, hosts, maids, and reception clerks to exceed the client's expectations.

That is what parents have been telling their children for generations – don't cut corners, don't slack off, be thorough, and do your best because you will never achieve true success through coincidences and shortcuts.

Yes, there are some areas where "good enough" is indeed good enough. You don't need to comb through all the hotel reviews to decide if you want to stay there, just as you don't need to pick up every single watermelon in the store to choose one. And you certainly don't need to watch all the episodes of every TV show out there because no one in history owes their success to the hours they spent in front of the TV.

But if you are pursuing some more challenging and vital achievements, watch out for some of the problems described in the Swiss Cheese Model and ensure that everything goes smoothly from start to finish, so you can get the results you want and be in control the entire time.

9 What Makes a True Professional?

You ask a room full of people, "Who here is afraid of flying?" and you're bound to get at least a few raised hands. Some wouldn't raise their hands but instead sink a little lower into their seat because the mere thought of flying makes them feel sick. They're easy to spot if you scan the crowd. Why would they be afraid? Well, voluntarily going into a metal tube of a few dozen or a few hundred tons and soaring to an altitude of 39,000 feet where the air is too thin to breathe, and the temperature is -76°F is not exactly people's natural state.

The obvious follow-up question: "If you answered you are afraid of flying, do you fly despite your fear?" The answer is always yes. What is it with these people? Are they crazy? People have been flying and will continue to fly to every corner of the Earth, some because they need to, others because they like it.

It's enough to look at people's faces at the airport to witness the full range of human emotion. They make a giant leap of faith getting on that plane, even though every fiber of their being tells them they shouldn't. People who have a fear of flying may fly once, twice, maybe even a hundred times, and they may even get used to it, but some small part of them will always be a little scared.

Can you imagine how much trust they put in the pilots and the rest of the crew?

If you ask a room full of people, "Who here is afraid of going to the doctor?" again, you'll get many raised hands. Who isn't afraid, at least a little? Who can stay calm when they have to walk up to a complete stranger, take off their clothes and tell that stranger the most private, intimate things about themselves, things they sometimes don't even share with those closest to them? It's not pleasant, but we all do it, don't we? We have to because we want to stay healthy. But the fear is always there.

If you look around a waiting room at people's faces, you'll again see a myriad of human emotions. But despite their fears, they all come to see the doctor. Do you realize how much trust they must have in doctors to do that?

> Can you imagine how much trust they put in the pilots and the rest of the crew?

How many people do we interact with? Consider the teller at the bank, your mechanic, construction workers, hair stylists, therapists, professors, and government officials, and many others. We entrust them with information to varying degrees about what we hold dearest, with the hope that they'll help us live a better life, be healthier or more attractive, earn more money or realize our dreams? And what would you call all those people? What makes them so unique that we choose them to improve or ease our lives? What do they all have in common that convinces us to put our trust in them? We consider them professionals. They must be if we trust them to do their job well.

Let's ask ourselves a few quick questions.

- Can we say the same thing about ourselves?
- How do we see ourselves in our place of work?
- Do other people trust us and our skills?
- Do we make other people's lives better or easier?

- Do we go home every day with the satisfaction of a job well done and a smile on our face?

What you do can either reinforce the trust that your coworkers or clients have in you or erode it completely. So, are we professionals?

What Is a Professional?

How do we define "professional"?

I got some of the most memorable definitions for what a professional is in my flight instructor course at the Airbus training center in Toulouse – APIC (Airbus Pilot Instructor Course). I was there with one of my coworkers, and we were the only two Romanians in a mixed group of French, Italian, German, Spanish, and Russian captains, all sent by our airlines for instructor training.

The course began at 9:00, and we were all advised not to be late. I was there as early as 8:00, and I was far from being the only one. We were all there, waiting for the course to begin, all nervous and excited. To our surprise, at 9:00, there was still no instructor in sight.

At 9:15, four people stumbled into the classroom. One of them said "good morning" and spent the next five minutes trying to get the projector to work. When he finally did, he immediately started running through what felt like hundreds of slides, chattering away in broken English with a heavy French accent. My colleagues and I were struggling to understand him.

Before the course, it had occurred to me that it might be one of those boring courses where an old geezer read from the presentation projected behind him. It may not have been that boring, but it wasn't good, either. The old-timer kept switching slides and unexpectedly changing the tone of his voice or trying different things, so we didn't lose focus, but it was hard to keep track of his line of thought.

A few minutes in, the instructor's phone rang, his ringtone loud and annoying. He stopped his slideshow and started rummaging in his bag's internal pocket, in his briefcase, under the papers on his chair, and back in his bag, where he finally found it but in a different pocket.

We thought he would turn it off, apologize, and carry on with the lecture, but no – he answered! He had a brief, hushed conversation with his back to us, after which he turned around and continued the lecture as if nothing had happened.

By this point, we were getting a little frustrated with how our morning was turning out. After all, we made it to Toulouse, to the largest aviation training center in the world, for *this*. We kept exchanging exasperated glances, hoping things would turn around soon. But the next thing we knew, one of the latecomers, who sat among us, suddenly stood up and shouted, "STOP!" The slideshow guy grinned at our confused faces. It had all been an act they had prepared for us, an exercise to analyze and from which to learn.

After we simmered down a bit and the instructors apologized for their ruse, they asked us what bothered us in their little show, and they listed our answers on a large flip chart hanging on a stand at the front of the class, titled "How to Be Professional." Throughout this introductory course, we must have filled a few dozens of these flip chart sheets, guided by our instructors, who hung up every sheet on the classroom walls to revisit it over the two weeks of the theory portion of the course before we started our simulator sessions.

Each person in the room had something to contribute to the chart. The instructors wrote down every observation, and next to it its solution, or rather, how a professional would approach each item.

Punctuality

The first thing people pointed out was the instructors' tardiness, of course. They told us to be there at 9:00, warned us not to be late, and then they were the ones who were late.

Pilots are control freaks when it comes to punctuality. It's almost an obsession.

Have you ever heard a pilot explain the takeoff will be late because we missed our slot? Every time we take off, we have a short window of time, the so-called "slot," assigned to us by the control tower so they can regulate the air traffic around the airport or in crowded airspaces. Delays put a lot of pressure on the crew.

> Pilots are control freaks when it comes to punctuality. It's almost an obsession.

We can miss our slot if:

- Anything goes wrong in the technical team's flight preparation
- A luggage carousel gets busted
- The catering doesn't show up on time
- The push-back truck breaks down
- We get any CAUTION lights in the cockpit after we turn on the engines
- An engineer has to come onboard to fix something
- Or any other snag we might hit in the complex procedure of preparing for takeoff

We could have a cascade of delays on our hands. These might even lead to the flight's cancellation. When we bear all this in mind, it's easy to understand why it's crucial for pilots to be on time and why we might expect the same from other people around us, in or outside the aviation industry.

Our first collective conclusion was that a professional is always punctual.

Introductions

The second thing we all pointed out was that the instructors did not introduce themselves. Even if we knew where we were and what was about to happen, and even though we could see their names on the screen, they were professionals, and they had to be both punctual and polite. When you first meet a business partner, they're going to want to know who and what you are. Whenever I fly with someone new, I always introduce them to the rest of the crew at the briefing. Even if we won't interact much during the flight, and we're usually separated by the flight deck's armored door, knowing their name and a few details about them helps build trust among us.

Our first collective conclusion was that a professional is always punctual.

Preparation

"The speaker wasn't prepared," many of us said. It took him a long time to get the projector to work, and he hadn't hooked up his computer to it, and he didn't have the relevant file at the ready. He spent a few good minutes feverishly looking through the course folder until he found the right one. It was like coming to a pre-flight briefing and having the commander kick it off with, "So what do we have here? Where are we going? Give me a minute to check the weather. Where's the weather file? Does anyone know where the plane is parked?"

As a captain, most of the time, I am the first person in the briefing room.

I can thoroughly read through the flight details and still have time to drink my coffee in peace. "A professional is always prepared," reads the sheet. If they're presenting, they should be the first person in the room and make sure that they have everything they need and that everything works.

As a captain, most of the time, I am the first person in the briefing room.

Set the Right Tone

"He jumped right into it," someone said. He didn't even try to interact with us or get to know us. He set a distance between us right from the start. The more people talked, the more we realized that it made us all feel uncomfortable, that our relationship with the instructor didn't set off on the right foot, and we didn't feel like a team.

No matter what your position is, how high up you are in the organization, you have to "sacrifice" at least a few minutes to set the right tone. Aside from the apparent benefit that happy workers are more productive, you also never know where the next critical piece of information might come from. It could even come from the newest and least experienced person on the team, as you saw in Chapter 7.

Good professionals, leaders, have to know their team, and how can you do that if you don't interact with them?

Rudeness

"His phone rang," some remarked. The ringtone was loud and irritating, and it went off for a good 15 seconds before he managed to find it. As if that wasn't enough of an interruption, he also took the call! "A professional would never do anything like that," we wrote on the flipchart.

How many examples of this can you think of? Some may be little, mundane things. In a different context, you wouldn't even notice them that much. We often let ourselves get distracted by the blinking notifications on our phones in the middle of a meeting. Sometimes we even answer. I can guarantee that your clients or coworkers do not appreciate this sort of behavior, and it might even make them judge you on how you present yourself professionally.

Communication Skills

"The presentation wasn't clear; he talked too fast and exaggerated his French accent, his English barely intelligible," I said. After a long, awkward pause, and a few exchanged looks between the instructors, I realized that he wasn't faking his accent – that was just the way he spoke. Luckily, the other instructors elegantly skipped over my remark.

This happened many years ago when I was a much younger pilot and hadn't yet been fully schooled in the art of communication and probably could've made my point a bit better. But I still think my observation was correct and relevant, even if it was offensive and his accent wasn't an intentional part of the act.

The way you talk, your enunciation, the rhythm and tone of your voice have a significant influence on how others perceive you, aside from the message you're trying to convey.

I have since learned this lesson and practice it every day.

Engagement

If I hadn't already royally screwed up with my first comment, I would have also pointed out that the instructor looked bored, as if this was his thousandth time teaching that course, and that he was only doing it because he "had to."

> The way you talk, your enunciation, the rhythm and tone of your voice have a significant influence on how others perceive you, aside from the message you're trying to convey.

I have fallen into that trap before, like many others, maybe even you. Sometimes it's the daily grind; other times, your personal life weighs you down. I have had days when I went to work, and I didn't feel like it. I did what I had to do without enjoying it, just going through the motions. I took off, I landed, and it didn't matter to me where, how, or with whom. I later realized that those days were the worst. I would go home completely wrecked and extremely dissatisfied.

But every time it happened, it was my choice to get on the plane – the place I spend most of my waking hours – without caring about how I spent my time there. This sort of attitude in the workplace not only affects your performance but may take a toll on your personal life. Most people don't have an ON/OFF switch with which they can make a smooth transition from SOUR, DISSATISFIED, and BORED mode to PLEASANT, EMPATHETIC, and ENERGIZED.

An excellent professional always finds a way to enjoy their work and care about what they do, even if it's completely routine.

I choose to care. From the pre-flight briefing, boarding, and my PA announcements, all the way through to the landing, I try my best to be there for the passengers. I want to know that the cabin's temperature is just right, or if something is bothering them, so that my colleagues and I can do everything we can to make the flight as comfortable and pleasant as possible. A good word or a cheerful PA announcement can work wonders, especially when we hit turbulence or if we're a few minutes late. Sometimes, as the passengers leave the plane, I let the kids into the cockpit. I try, and most of the time, I succeed in putting a smile on their faces, no matter how tired I am.

> An excellent professional always finds a way to enjoy their work and care about what they do, even if it's completely routine.

Too Much Information

We also told the instructor that he bombarded us with too much information. The 860 slides he started reading to us were too detailed and too hard to follow. In the end, it's no use being punctual, prepared, and polite if you're not actually good at what you do.

Common Qualities of Professionals

Professionals have many other characteristics, aside from those we've already listed. What's interesting and important to point out is that they're pretty much universal and are valid for any domain or industry, maybe with a few variations.

People who are known as genuine professionals all share many of the same traits. Similarly, those considered weak professionals share a lot of the same characteristics. Often, we make the distinction using the same criteria. Where the former has "good" or "excellent" marks, the latter would receive an "insufficient."

How do you define yourself in your place of work? How do others view you concerning what you do, day in and day out? If we all think of ourselves as professionals, we surely can't ignore those few fundamental characteristics common in all trades. If we delve deeper into the matter, we'll find four traits we can extrapolate from the pool of fundamental requirements. If you really want to be in control every day, you should work on them. How do you score on each one?

1. Professionals Are Not Only Masters of Their Craft But Are Also Well Versed in Its History.

If you read on, you'll see that the next three items on our list are requirements and habits you can adopt right now because they're all about current activity. This first one, though, is a prerequisite, a thing you should have already done if you call yourself a professional, which is a title you cannot claim to have unless you've studied your trade and its history. You can choose many titles for yourself – enthusiast, amateur, student, apprentice – or any other way you may choose to describe your journey.

You're only at the destination, being a professional, when you genuinely master everything that came before you.

You're only at the destination, being a professional, when you genuinely master everything that came before you.

If you have, that doesn't mean that you stop learning. You never stop learning. But here are three things you don't see professionals do, and they're all part of this first prerequisite.

A. True Professionals Don't Reinvent the Wheel Every Single Time.

They know where to find the wheel, what to do with it, and they might even think about ways to improve it – more on this later – but they do not waste time making from scratch what their profession already has. Instead, they first check to see whether someone has already found a solution to their problem.

B. True Professionals Do Not Take Credit for Somebody Else's Work, Claiming to Have Invented the Wheel Themselves.

They do not act like they're the first to do what they do. They're modest, and they know their place; they know they're the tenth, the hundredth, or the thousandth generation in their field. They're just happy to be there, get good at what they do, and be useful to those around.

C. True Professionals Never Get Caught Not Knowing What They Are Expected to Know.

They are familiar with everything that came before them, they studied everything there was to learn, and even if they can't quote from "the book," they are well prepared. If they make a mistake, it's because the job is complicated and ever-changing, not because they didn't do their homework.

Professionals have a vast arsenal of knowledge and experience. When it's an argument between someone outside the profession – an amateur – and a professional, it is not a matter of opinion. Even if it were, it would be a breeze for the professional because they have equipped themselves with everything we mentioned. An amateur's opinion comes up against experience accumulated over decades or even centuries, against shared knowledge from every corner of the Earth, of anyone who has ever taken part in the profession.

Do you see why there's no competition? In many fields, an amateur vs. professional would be akin to a soccer game between a kindergarten class and the national team at the World Cup. Only they would stand even less of a chance to win.

Do you see what a shame it would be, now more than ever, for anyone who calls themselves a professional to disregard the treasure at their fingertips? Let me take it a step further: Can you imagine the risks companies take when they leave decisions on professional matters up to clueless executives and not the people who actually practice that profession?

So, what do you think? Are there people who fail that first test? They may not be amongst our readership, but they're out there. They exist in any trade, from old professions with long-standing traditions to newer ones where there are virtually no prerequisites such as a high school diploma, an entrance exam, or a certification by a recognized institution. This typically happens in newer titles like manager, marketer, salesperson, real estate agent, consultant, coach, software developer, and many others. Those practicing these vocations could probably rise to professional status, couldn't they?

2. Professionals Have High Standards

The third part of this book is dedicated to methods that help you stay in control so you can always get the best results – not just "sometimes" or when the planets align – and be able to perform well under (a reasonable amount of) pressure.

The first requirement is a solid foundation on which you can rely and continue building your professional identity in the long run.

The world is full of people who know their stuff and hope that they can get by on that alone and even achieve success. That is never the case. Success, control, confidence, and performance require a lot of work every day and a constant effort to give your all to become the best.

Daily Tasks

What does "high standard" even mean? In short, it means repeating the same three tasks every day:

1. Do the little things well
2. Do the big things well
3. Always look for something to add to both categories

> The first requirement is a solid foundation on which you can rely and continue building your professional identity in the long run.

The little things are the solutions to all the mistakes my instructors in Toulouse made intentionally – keeping promises, being early, being prepared, and many others, specific or nonspecific to any one profession. Our conclusion regarding those was that it would be a shame to be good at all the little stuff if you're not actually good at your job. But even the best specialists in the world would quickly ruin their reputation if they didn't sweat the little things. Especially today, the tiniest detail out of place can easily become common knowledge that grows and spreads like wildfire, leaving nothing but destruction in its wake.

You won't ruin your reputation by being late once, but you have to be careful. Why would people want to work with someone who's either chronically late, unprepared, repeatedly forgets their names or needs a reminder of the project's purpose? It does not necessarily mean that the professionals in question aren't good at their job, but most people would prefer someone who's proficient at the little things as well as the big ones. Perhaps you've met people like that, who may be very skilled at their craft but are very difficult or annoying to work with. There's a limit to what people are willing to swallow when dealing with "stars" and their whims, and they might put their foot down faster and harder than said "star" would expect.

The big things mean being ethical and passionate about your job.

Too many people take shortcuts for money, comfort, or because they just don't care enough to be thorough. And too many people do their jobs well but have become like robots, doing everything on autopilot, which makes them prone to serious mistakes.

When are drivers most likely to be involved in an accident? It is not when they're driving on a new road in a new country. That's when they're most focused. They even turn off the radio and tell their passengers to keep it down so they can concentrate on which turn to take next. They are much more likely to have an accident on their way home, on a route they've driven thousands of times over the years and which does not require any of their attention. They don't see a YIELD sign where previously they had the right of way. Without passion or concentration, without caring enough to be mentally present, it's hard to be in control, hold yourself to high standards, and make people believe in your profession.

The big things mean being ethical and passionate about your job.

And lastly, what does "Always look for things to add" mean? It means aspiring to become even better with each passing day. Do some reading, follow your colleagues' work, and learn from them. Analyze what you did, what you could have done better, and what you will do in the future in a similar situation. Never stop investing in yourself; never stop growing. That is the main thing you can do to improve your life and the lives of the people around you.

3. Professionals Respect Their Clients

How many professionals have you had to deal with who ticked all the boxes so far, only to fail miserably at this third one? Some professionals get caught up in their work. They're so absorbed in it that they forget they're not the only people in the world and that their efforts should first and foremost serve others.

Who Are the Clients?

For pilots, the clients are the passengers, who have the right to travel as comfortably as possible. Their clients are also the airlines, who have the right to have trustworthy captains who take care of the increasingly expensive aircraft lent to them by the airlines, who also depend on their captains to keep their reputations intact.

For architects, the client is the construction company that's going to build the building and the people who are going to use it after its completion. You can also call the people passing by that building every day clients. After all, they have to look at it. You may even count the city, which depends on its buildings to make it more appealing, as the architect's client.

We all have clients. You should avoid people who think they only work for themselves – for ambition or to prove something, to gain something. These people see clients as nothing more than a necessary evil who should be thankful that the "professionals" even tolerate them.

What Do Professionals Do?

What do real professionals do? They listen and communicate openly and honestly. Dedicated professionals are doctors who don't just go through as many patients as possible on a busy day but who take the time to explain what and where the problem is. In more challenging cases, they provide encouragement and valuable advice for the people around the patient as well. They are those who, after a successful operation, smile and are genuinely happy for the patient's family instead of coldly retreating to the "staff only" zones.

Did the instructors at the Toulouse training center have respect for us, their "clients"? Judging by the first few minutes, it would be a big fat NO, but we soon discovered the situation was different. Their effort to simulate a catastrophic start to the course to stimulate a memorable discussion, risking their reputations in the process, came from the will to help us. And it was a lot more helpful than dryly going through a list of things of what to do and what not to do as a professional. It was so memorable that, fifteen years later, I use it here as an example. It would have been much simpler for them to give us a checklist and say, "Be professional," but it wouldn't have had the same impact. I wouldn't have held onto the lesson it imparted for this long.

Professionals do not exist in a vacuum. Worrying about the client – whoever they may be – is what makes the whole thing work and moves things forward. That is why real professionals start their workday thinking about the client and what they could do for them. And they continue their day the same way, as a professional should.

4. Professionals Make Their Profession a Little Better

Based on their interaction with you, what impression would you say people have of your profession after they've met you? As professionals, our goal should be to make our clients believe in what we do a little more every time. To this end, think of the requirements I've listed above as legs in a four-legged base – take one away, and the entire thing is unstable. This is the final one, and it is arguably the most important.

Firstly, it implies constant reflection on what needs to be improved, asking ourselves how we can make things better, have a more significant impact, save on resources, or use alternative resources altogether.

Constant Improvement

Firstly, it implies constant reflection on what needs to be improved, asking ourselves how we can make things better, have a more significant impact, save on resources, or use alternative resources altogether.

People call professionals in both to administer and implement solutions that others initiated and to make their contribution to the trade, advancing and transforming it. If no one ever did that, we'd be living in a very different world. This book gave you a sneak peek at how every incident, accident, or a captain's unusual experience provides an opportunity to make aviation safer, faster, and more efficient.

As a professional in your trade, you have the same opportunity. What can you improve? What innovation can you bring to the table?

It's not a coincidence that this is the last item on our list. Some people barely begin their career, and already they want to change their profession on their second day on the job, if possible. These newcomers claim that most of the people in their profession are past their prime, unable to keep up with the times, the technology, the clients' demands, and that the profession is lucky to have them, the unexpected saviors. The newcomers who know better than anyone what to do. You can put innovative ideas on the table, and it is good practice. Still, to follow through with innovation – how to do it, what to change, where to start – you must have a deep understanding of the profession and everything around it to understand what to cut out and what to add. Many of the greatest innovators in history only got to their "Eureka" moment because they knew their industry inside out.

Secondly, this requirement assumes that real professionals do not hesitate to share their knowledge with their peers.

They don't hold anything back; they pass whatever they learned from their experience onto others. They aim to groom their colleagues. And they don't make them in their image, either; they help their fellow professionals form their own identity.

True professionals – an expression we've often used in this chapter to distinguish them from people who only have a title but who do not check these boxes – measure their value not through the results they got for themselves but through the impact they had on their environment, the profession, colleagues, and clients.

Secondly, this requirement assumes that real professionals do not hesitate to share their knowledge with their peers.

How do you see your standing in your profession if you examine it through these four prisms?

We went into so much detail and thoroughly discussed what it takes to be a real professional for two reasons. One is because if you do everything we described above, it will make your life infinitely easier and more straightforward and allow you more freedom. The other is that we are all ambassadors of our profession, and we should all strive to make the best possible impression, no matter what our job is. So, do everything in your power to be a good ambassador. If everyone did that, the world would be a much better place.

Epilogue | How Does Your Plane Fly? The Four Forces

You must have asked yourself how planes fly, right? You're obviously in good company. The most renowned scientists not only asked themselves how "a machine heavier than air" could ever lift off the ground, but for many years, even mere seconds before the first plane took off, many of them insisted that it was physically impossible.

In many ways, we can understand their perspective because 60, 100, or 500 tons of steel flying over oceans and continents at 620 mph like a flock of jacked-up geese negates all reason, doesn't it? Some call it a miracle, and there sure is something a little miraculous about flying, but the truth entails a lot less magic and a lot more physics. It's impressive, fancy physics – but physics, nonetheless. At this very moment, as you're reading this, up to 30,000 planes are in the air, making up to 200,000 flights transporting about 10 million people every day.

Aviation has come a long way since the first flight took place a little over a century ago, or since Churchill's first trip back from America, when he almost crashed the plane. He got chilly on the way and decided to have a little onboard bonfire to warm up, setting the aircraft ablaze.

Nowadays, you can comfortably make the 4,500-nautical-mile journey from Bucharest to America in eight hours. Some flights, called Extra Long Range, last 16 or even 18 hours, connecting remote cities on different continents, traveling up to 8,500 nautical miles at a time, meaning a little over 15,500 kilometers!

Even if you are a frequent flier, and flying has become somewhat of a habit for you, give yourself a minute to appreciate what a miracle it is that we're able to do what ancient civilizations only dreamed of. I, for one, have that thought every time I take off. Beyond the SOP, the standard calls, and the operation manuals, what I do is wonderful and unique, and I feel lucky that I get to fly every day.

What Keeps Planes Up

There is one question I always ask candidates interviewing for pilot positions: "How do planes fly?"

The candidates are almost always surprised by this. They expect all sorts of complicated questions on aerodynamics, and they're even more surprised when I ask them to draw and explain it in a way that a high school student could quickly grasp. You'd be surprised by how many of them fail this basic exercise, which should be elementary for any pilot. Needless to say, as far as I'm concerned, such pilots have no business being in an airline cockpit.

There is one question I always ask candidates interviewing for pilot positions: "How do planes fly?"

In a nutshell, a plane flies because the shape of its wings causes air to move faster over the wing than it does under it. The airstream splits at the front part of the wing – named leading edge – which is the first to make contact with the air as the wing moves forward. In contrast, the difference between the lower air pressure above the wing and the higher air pressure below it generates lift and pushes it upwards. The faster the air stream is, the greater the difference in air pressure and the greater the lift.

Wing Shape

Of course, I hold my candidates to a slightly higher standard – for example, I expect them to tell me that there are a few more forces at play in generating lift under the wings. Imagine the shape of a water drop, now rotate it 90°, so it's horizontal, elongated, with both ends slightly curved downwards. That's how the cross-sections look on the wings of any plane. The force system I'm about to describe is roughly the same one you'd find in many other everyday devices like fans, compressors, and propeller blades on aeronautical engines.

Four Critical Forces

Lift

Let's use this image of the wing cross-sections – that elongated horizontal water drop shape – to demonstrate the four forces that affect any surface in motion, resulting in lift – the force that keeps the plane airborne and makes flight possible.

Thrust

The most important force is thrust. Without thrust, there would be no movement or airflow. This force moves the plane forward, and as it gets stronger, the wing's speed grows, increasing the difference between the air pressure below the wing and the air pressure above the wing.

Drag

Wind resistance or drag opposes thrust and "cancels out" the wings' motion forward, which pushes the plane back. Any object moving through a fluid is subjected to drag, the intensity of which depends, among other things, on the object's shape. The boxier the shape, the more drag it's going to generate when it moves.

Weight

Another obstacle for flying is an object's weight, which is a force that always pulls it down.

The engineer designing the plane has to plan the shape and surface of the wings so that at a certain level of thrust, they generate enough lift to overpower the plane's weight and drag. For example, a jet aircraft engine weighing about 65 tons generates about 120,000 horsepower, which is the thrust needed to achieve the necessary lift for the aircraft to fly. This is the balance, the play between the four forces.

Now I wouldn't want you to look at drag and weight like "the enemy," because as strange as it may seem, you need all four forces to fly.

Balancing the Four Forces

Now I wouldn't want you to look at drag and weight like "the enemy," because as strange as it may seem, you need all four forces to fly.

Without weight (or gravity), the plane wouldn't be able to glide, and without resistance, the plane wouldn't be able to stop unless we had runways of at least 6 miles at every airport. The manipulation and control of these four forces make it possible to take off, fly, cruise, and land safely.

Would you be interested in a third and final drawing inside this book or on a paper next to your ebook? If yes, you're welcome to use the space provided here.

Start by drawing a plane. Now, that might be easier said than done, but I'm confident you can pull it off. Imagine you're in a plane and you look outside the window and you see another plane at the same level as you are, flying in the same direction as your plane. Let's say the plane is flying from left to right as you look at this page or at your paper. It's practically a long horizontal rectangle, with a round end at the right, actually quite a pointy one – be sure to draw the windows of the cockpit – and at the left end the bottom horizontal line of the rectangle comes up at an angle to meet the top line. Remember to place a fin on top of the plane at the left end. Should you draw the wings? Well, yes, you could try. Start at the middle of a plane and go a little backwards with a line. That will be fine. If you want, you can add the engine(s), the windows, the doors but you can just as well move on to drawing the 4 arrows.

Here are the four forces now. Draw four arrows around the plane, each about an inch long:

- An arrow to the right, horizontally. Start from the cockpit. Write Thrust on top of it.
- An arrow to the left, horizontally. Start from the left end of the plane and move towards the left edge of your page. Write Drag on top of the arrow.
- An arrow downward. Start right below the plane, more or less in the middle. Write Weight next to it.

- An arrow upward. Start right above the plane, also in the middle. Write Lift next to it.

No matter how many times I see the drawing with the four forces – thrust, lift, drag, and weight – I can't help but think about how I fly. I make an analogy between the aerodynamic diagram and my professional life, and I ask myself every time what makes me fly.

The Will to Fly

How do the four forces affect me? What inspires me to get up at 4:00 AM and leave home with a smile on my face at the thought of flying, regardless of the destination – Cluj-Napoca, Tenerife, Sofia, or New York – dark cockpit or no?

To this day, I remember the serious talk I had with my parents, in which I told them I didn't know how I was ever going to finish high school. How could I wake up every day at 7:00 AM? You could tell by looking at their faces that they were thinking the same thing – they knew me.

I did manage to finish high school in the end, but only my mom can tell you about the daily battles of getting me out of bed and out the door in time for school. I would ride my bike like a madman, and I almost always came into class a few minutes late. Back then, I didn't know I would become a pilot. It was just a distant dream. The future was a big blob of uncertainty. This is when I identified the first of my four forces, the "weight" that was pulling me down: *comfort.*

Then I enlisted in the military, which was the only way you could become a pilot back in those days. Finally, I had a horizon by which to navigate – I was going to be a pilot, which became my *thrust.*

For four years, I woke up at 5:30 AM every single day. How did I pull it off? After all, I was the same person who said he wouldn't graduate because he couldn't stand getting up so early! I practically threw myself out of bed and dragged myself to class every day. My thrust then overpowered my *weight*, and it was clear to me that I would only have to put up with it for four years, at the end of which I would achieve my dream and become a pilot.

Drag? There was no shortage of that. Military life was entirely new for me: the constant lack of privacy in a dorm room of ten people, the rules, the ranks, the uniform, and guard duty, sometimes the stress, which only seemed to get worse the closer we were to the end, probably because we were so eager to be done with it already. But with it all, I had *lift* – the joy of flying. I've been obsessed with flying ever since I was a little kid, and even now, I stop and look at planes whenever I see them in the sky above.

But all that is in the past. What makes me fly today?

The lift hasn't changed; that much is clear – the miracle of flight. I cannot shut up about my job, and if I happen to meet a fellow pilot at a party, we're sure to ruin it for everyone, rambling on and on about LEAP engines, the newest plane models, and the unending rivalry between Airbus and Boeing. I love my job, and I think that is an indispensable motivation for any professional in any field.

Sometimes I get invitations to speak in front of groups of

professionals who have nothing to do with aviation. At first, I was surprised to learn how many similarities there were between the different trades, common ground between all walks of life: banking, medicine, international corporations in other industries, etc. When I finish, people come up to me, and aside from appreciating the similarities between us professionals, our approach to different problems, and our procedures, I recognize in them the same passion – their lift.

I have long since defeated the force that had kept me from getting out of bed – my teenage "weight" – but it has since taken the form of worries, bills, other personal issues, and daily uncertainty that have nothing to do with flying but try to keep me from taking to the sky. I have flown on Christmas, New Year's Eve, my kids' birthdays, or when they were sick. I've flown with an entire crew biting their nails with worry for the airline's future. Still, every time I closed the door to the plane, I took off leaving everything behind me.

Our will to do our job – the mission we have to accomplish, and in the best way possible – outweighs any concern.

Our will to do our job – the mission we have to accomplish, and in the best way possible – outweighs any concern.

Some people's thrust is the need to make a living while, for others, it's duty or praise. Some have a strong will to become better professionals. For many, it may be a mixture of all of the above. My thrust is almost always the thought of heading out to the airport with a smile on my face, eager to set the engines to full speed. Apart from that, I've always thought at least a part of my thrust is my ambition to be one of the best. It's why I spend every day trying to learn something from everyone around me.

My drag, the things that keep me from moving forward too fast, are the rules, the SOPs, and the bureaucracy, every safety restriction, every one of those 61 signatures through which I assume responsibility, and every page in the logbook – the ATL (Aircraft Technical Log). We pilots sometimes joke that every 30-minute flight precedes 30 more minutes of paperwork.

The forces that drive us may change, as well as the balance between them. Some days we feel motivated by one thing or another. Still, as professionals, we need to remember our goals and to know that our thrust and lift will always be enough to get us off the ground, no matter how hard it gets or how many limits and restrictions we have to work around.

What makes you fly?

Index of Aviation Terms

A/THR – AUTO THRUST

A system that automatically regulates the engine power, depending on the speed the pilot has selected. It ensures the engines keep a steady pace within the allowed limits, preventing the plane from going over the maximum or under a certain minimum speed.

AP – AUTO PILOT

An automated system that keeps the plane in a specified vertical and horizontal flight modes. These systems can be as simple as a heading and vertical speed or more complex navigation systems that keep the plane on a specific route and directed towards a landing strip.

APIC – AIRBUS PILOT INSTRUCTOR COURSE

Flight-instructor training organized by the Airbus Training Centre in Toulouse.

ATC – AIR TRAFFIC CONTROL

An umbrella name for all the people and institutions involved in directing aircraft traffic, from controllers directing planes as they taxi to the control tower and other institutions that monitor and direct air traffic around airports or on flight routes.

ATL – AIRCRAFT TECHNICAL LOG

A logbook that includes the CRS, as well as lists of minor defects with which the plane is permitted to fly, or signs of wear and tear (and the deadlines for fixing them), but also a record of all the maintenance activity commanders or technical personnel did on previously reported defects. The ATL must be aboard the plane at all times.

ATTENTION! CABIN CREW AT STATIONS!

A warning the commander gives through the PA (Public Address) to the cabin crew in emergency situations for which there is no time to prepare: for example, when the plane is on final approach or after an aborted takeoff. In those moments, the flight attendants do a Silent Review, ready for emergency evacuation if need be.

BACKTRACK

A ground maneuver in which the aircraft taxis to the end of the runway and makes a 180° turn to take off, using the entire length of the runway.

BRACE/BRACE FOR IMPACT

A command given by either the commander or the chief purser in case of an impending forced landing, calling passengers and crew to assume the position explained in the emergency briefing before takeoff. Your best chance of avoiding injury in case of violent acceleration or deceleration is that position: Place your arms over your head and fold your body over your legs.

CABIN CREW TAKE YOUR SEATS FOR TAKEOFF / LANDING
A command the commander gives on the PA to the flight attendants to inform them of takeoff or landing and to tell them to start their Silent Review.

CABIN SECURE FOR TAKE-OFF/LANDING
A report the Chief Purser gives the Commander, meaning all passengers are in their seats with seatbelts fastened. Without it, the plane cannot initiate takeoff or landing.

CALM CAVOK 1013
An expression pilots use to describe perfect weather for flying. It is calm wind, ceiling and visibility OK, standard 1,013 millibar atmospheric pressure.

CAT – CLEAR AIR TURBULENCE
Invisible turbulent areas, potentially dangerous because there is no way to detect them, no clouds or other weather indicators. They are marked on the weather maps in the preflight briefing file. They are caused by collisions of air masses or strong winds at cruising altitude, between 4,350 miles and 7,456 miles, or when wind hits high mountain peaks nearby.

CAUTION/CAUTION LIGHT
Informs the pilot of minor malfunctions that do not require immediate attention.

CHARLIE-BRAVO/CB
Cumulonimbus clouds, which can sometimes form a vertical cloud mass measuring up to 9,320 miles and typically indicate thunderstorms, severe turbulence, precipitation, etc. Flying through them is strictly forbidden.

CHIEF PURSER

The chief flight attendant. Responsibilities include overseeing the flight attendants, completing reports, communicating with passengers, and verifying all safety procedures are followed. The chief purser is knowledgeable about the aircraft, communications, and emergency procedures. This person is third in command in case the two pilots are incapacitated.

COMMANDER

Also called captain, the commander is the pilot who's legally in charge of everything that happens on board from the moment the doors to the plane close for takeoff to when they reopen after landing. The commander may sit in the jump seat, in which case the PIC sits on the left, and the F/O sits on the right.

COPILOT/FIRST OFFICER (F/O)

Originally a navy term meaning second-in-command after the captain, and in the context of aviation, meaning copilot. This is a professional pilot, certified to fly that type of plane, who can step in if the commander is incapacitated. This pilot is lower in the hierarchy and experience level than the captain.

CROSSCHECK AND REPORT/ARM AND CROSSCHECK

Commands the chief purser gives the cabin crew over the PA to disarm "crosscheck and report" or arm "arm and crosscheck" the emergency slides from the doors or the evacuation hatches in case of an emergency evacuation. Opening the doors when the slides are armed triggers them to automatically deploy in a matter of seconds, which in itself can cause a serious accident. This can happen if the flight attendant operating the emergency slide is not careful enough to correctly position the arming handles, and the door opens on the ladder or on the boarding bridge at the airport.

CRS – CERTIFICATE OF RELEASE TO SERVICE

A document that declares the aircraft fit for operation. It is issued the first time the aircraft is cleared for use and after every major maintenance, either for repairs or periodical inspections.

CVR – COCKPIT VOICE RECORDER

A complex system that records all the sounds in the cockpit, part of the black box.

DE-ICING

The process of removing snow or ice from the exterior surfaces of the plane, including the fuselage, wings, tail, engines, or the surface of the runway.

DOWN 3 GREEN

A quick confirmation (in some types of aircraft) of the landing gear's correct position before touching down on the runway.

EMERGENCY LANDING

Priority landing following an emergency that might endanger a flight or when there's an emergency on board the plane where a passenger or a member of the crew requires immediate medical attention.

ETOPS – EXTENDED TWIN OPERATION

A set of rules for flying double-engine aircraft over long stretches of uninhabited land or water to ensure the flight's completion even if one of the engines fails.

FD - FLIGHT DIRECTOR

The primary means of guiding the aircraft with the help of two perpendicular bars on the screens in front of the pilots. The vertical bar is used to set the plane's trajectory (heading, route, etc.), and the horizontal bar is used to set the vertical profile of the plane (nose turned up for takeoff or down for landing, for example).

FDP - FLIGHT DUTY PERIOD

The time between reporting for duty at the airport and parking the plane at the gate after landing.

FDR - FLIGHT DATA RECORDING

A complex system that monitors and records all flight parameters (speed, altitude, pitch, pressure, etc.) and data from all the systems of the aircraft, including the CVR. This is popularly known as the Black Box.

FFS- FULL FLIGHT SIMULATOR

A highly technical room, usually about 10 feet high, 10 feet long and 10 feet wide. It is suspended on 6 hydraulic jacks. The simulator accurately recreates the actual cockpit environment and everything that might happen in flight, from everyday situations to emergency scenarios. The simulator allows pilots to see, hear, and feel everything as if they were on a real airborne plane. It is used for training and testing pilots.

FINAL APPROACH

The final landing procedure, closest to the runway, when the plane is aligned with the landing strip.

FL – FLIGHT LEVEL

A term used in aviation and aeronautical meteorology. The flight level is the plane's altitude expressed in hundreds of feet when the altimeter is set to a standard atmospheric pressure of 1,013 millibars. For example, FL100 means 10,000 feet, which is about 3,050 meters.

FLIGHT DECK/COCKPIT

The room at the front tip of the plane where the pilots sit.

FLIGHT TIME

Time spent flying from the moment the plane takes off the ground until it touches down at the destination.

FORCED LANDING

When a pilot must land at an unfamiliar location, sometimes without a landing strip, because of major malfunctions in the aircraft: double engine failure, damage to hydraulics system and landing gear, etc. As long as they're still in control of the aircraft, the pilots will try to land on a clear surface on land or water, as safely as possible, so as not to cause death or injury to anyone.

GALLEY

The plane's kitchen, the area where the crew prepares the onboard service. It has ovens, coffee makers, and storage for food and beverages.

GO AROUND

The standard procedure for an aborted landing, also known as "missed approach," for which there could be several reasons, from an obstruction on the runway, such as another unauthorized aircraft or animals, to a lack of visual cues in cases of reduced visibility.

HOLDING

The state of circling the destination airport, used for queuing the planes for landing.

IATA – INTERNATIONAL AIR TRANSPORT ASSOCIATION

Around 80% of all airlines in the world are members of IATA.

ICAO – INTERNATIONAL CIVIL AVIATION ORGANIZATION

A United Nations agency specialized in global aeronautical regulation.

ILS – INSTRUMENT LANDING SYSTEM

A complex radio navigation system that automatically guides the planes onto the runway. It consists of two or more stations located on the ground near the runway, employing radio beams to guide planes in the right direction and to the correct landing slope, and horizontal beacons to guide them towards the runway. The system is exact, and it allows planes to land safely, even under conditions of extremely poor visibility. Some systems are so accurate that if the plane is equipped for it, and the crew has the necessary qualifications, it is possible to make a **zero** landing – visibility zero meter and ceiling zero, dense fog.

JUMP SEAT

A chair (or chairs) in the cockpit reserved for observer-pilots or instructors, other than the two chairs used by the pilots actively flying the plane.

JUST CULTURE

An organizational model that sets out to find the causes for subpar performance rather than guilty parties. This philosophy emphasizes that people make mistakes because of faults in a system's design. The main question that should be asked in such cases is "What didn't work as it should have in the system?" and not "Whose fault is it?"

MILE/NM – NAUTICAL MILE

Takes its name from Latin (**mille passus** – a thousand steps), measuring at 1,150 miles or 1,852 meters. Sailors use this unit to measure distance, equal to 1/60 of a meridian on longitude 0, measured at its intersection with the equator.

NON-PUNISHMENT ENVIRONMENT

See JUST CULTURE, an environment that encourages voluntary reporting of errors or digressions in the interest of improving procedures.

NOTAM – NOTICE TO AIRMEN

Announcements made by aeronautical authorities about potential dangers around airports or along flight routes.

PA – PUBLIC ADDRESSING

A communication system comprised of speakers placed throughout the cabin, through which the commander and the chief purser communicate messages to the passengers or the crew.

PIC – PILOT IN COMMAND

The commander who may also be referred to as the captain. The PIC usually sits on the left.

PILOT

A member of the aircrew qualified to fly that type of plane in the role of both copilot and captain, depending on qualifications and experience level.

PILOT FLYING

The pilot actively flying the plane at a given moment, responsible for safely flying and navigating the plane.

PITCH

The angle between a plane's longitudinal axis and the horizon.

PNF/PM – PILOT NON-FLYING/PILOT MONITORING

In charge of communication and monitoring the plane's flight trajectory and the plane's systems.

PURSER/SENIOR CABIN CREW

The Chief Purser, third-in-command in case the two pilots are incapacitated.

PUSHBACK TRUCK

Specialized equipment for pushing planes out of their parking spot. Theoretically, any aircraft can back up by itself, and some do – mainly those with propellers and turboprops. The problem with jet planes backing up independently is that they would require a lot of power, and the resulting strong hot air streams would obliterate the platform and pull objects into the engines, which could damage or even destroy them.

QRH – QUICK REFERENCE HANDBOOK

Generally known as a checklist, a collection of procedures for routine and emergency situations that may occur in every one of the aircraft's systems. It contains a list of tables and procedures to follow to calculate the aircraft's performance when the plane's computer malfunctions. It also contains the so-called normal checklist, a list of maneuvers and things to hook up before or after each stage of the flight, before and after turning the engines on, before takeoff, before ascending to cruising altitude, before landing, before parking, etc. The checklists are printed out, written in black on white in regular characters (not everything is in capital letters), so they are easy and fast to read. They are read and confirmed out loud. There are two kinds of checklists: "Challenge and Response" for normal situations and "Read and Do" for abnormal or emergency situations.

SECOND OFFICER

A copilot in training, who plays a minor and limited role in the cockpit. A second officer might operate the controls at cruising altitudes but is in the jump seat for most stages of the flight.

SEVERE TURBULENCE

Turbulence is considered severe when unsecured objects start flying through the cabin and the cockpit. The overhead compartment doors burst open, and the flight instruments are hard to read. Unfortunately, it is not uncommon to experience severe turbulence, and it can seriously harm passengers or crew members who are standing in the aisle. Still, it rarely hurts people who are sitting down with their seatbelts fastened.

SHARKLETS

The name Airbus gave to the little wings on top of the tips of the plane's wings, which help reduce drag and save on fuel.

SILENT REVIEW

A mental state of preparation for unpredictable emergency situations, which flight attendants go into during every takeoff and landing. They go over the emergency evacuation procedure in their heads, evaluating the passengers sitting next to the emergency exits in terms of how capable they are to execute emergency procedures if push comes to shove.

SLOT

The narrow window of time assigned by air traffic controllers for any commercial flight to take off, either because it's peak hour or because the specific runway is particularly crowded, or because of difficult weather conditions that force many planes to crowd together in the same area.

SOP – STANDARD OPERATING PROCEDURE

A set of step-by-step instructions for a correct, complete, and efficient execution of complex procedures that are a part of a pilot's day-to-day work. Every SOP starts with a standard call.

STANDARD CALL

An integral part of any SOP, a standard call is standardized communication created to reduce misunderstandings in the cockpit. It can be the simple act of announcing an action or a maneuver, a command to the PNF, or commands that initiate emergency protocols, but the receiving party always confirms to eliminate miscommunications.

STATION COPY

A certificate that attests to the pilot receiving the aircraft and then inspecting and clearing it for flight. The certificate stays on the ground with the other liability forms the commander has signed.

STERILE COCKPIT

The concept of restricting or prohibiting any conversations or actions in the cockpit that are not strictly related to the flight. It's usually used under FL100 – around 10,000 feet.

TAXI

The plane's movement on the ground.

THRUST

Engine power, the force that pushes the plane forward.

TURBULENCE

Caused mostly by weather phenomena that bring about sharp changes in the direction and intensity of the wind, but it can also be caused by vortex created by large airplanes (wake turbulence). The most common occurrence of turbulence is in storm clouds, cumulonimbus (CB), which the naked eye can see or are easily detectable with the onboard radar, as it is a mass of ice and water.

TYPE RATING

Pilot certification course for a specific type of plane, comprising ground training, simulator sessions, flight training, and supervised flights.

TYPE RATING EXAMINER (TRE)

A pilot commander in charge of testing pilots in training who are at the end of their Type Rating course or other advanced programs (qualifying for captain or instructor, for example) and, depending on national and international legislation, has the authority to certify or flunk a pilot for that qualification. The type rating examiner also extends pilots' type rating in simulator sessions as part of routine training. They also have all the same legal privileges as a TRI.

TYPE RATING INSTRUCTOR (TRI)

A pilot-instructor charged with preparing professional pilots for qualifying on a particular type of plane. Similarly, the TRI prepares pilots in flight or on the simulator and recommends them for TRE examinations as part of their routine annual training.

V1

The maximum speed a plane can reach during takeoff and still be able to stop safely on the runway. Pilots calculate V1 before every takeoff, accounting for the runway's elevation, length, and, if necessary, level of contamination, wind speed and direction, atmospheric pressure, temperature, the plane's mass, and minor defects with which the plane has clearance to fly. (Level of contamination refers to ice, snow, water, rubber or other substances on the runway.)

Pilots are trained to take their hands off the control column once the plane reaches V1, so they are not tempted to stop the takeoff. This may sound counterintuitive, but most of the time, once the plane reaches V1, it is better for it to take off than try to brake on the runway. This holds true even if there are major problems, like an engine fire. The immediate question (and the instinct you, the pilot, have to fight) is if you can make it off the runway with the fire a few seconds after the warning starts beeping and try to take out the fire in flight, and then land back safely.

The answer is always YES because otherwise, the already scary scenario of an engine fire (which you can handle with the equipment you have on board) might turn into an even more frightening nightmare, like skidding off the runway, with the risk of destroying both the plane and the runway, not to mention hurting people.

V ROT

Rotation speed, the speed at which the plane leaves the ground, greater or equal to V1.

V2

Safe takeoff speed, calculated to ensure takeoff even if one engine fails.

VISUAL APPROACH

A landing procedure that requires the approval of the control tower. It's only done in conditions of excellent visibility (over 3,100 feet meters), where the only instruments the pilot uses to land are the watch (chronometer), compass, and altimeter.

WARNING

A cockpit alert informing the pilots of a major malfunction that requires their immediate attention.

About the Authors

Emil Dobrovolschi is a pilot, a pilot instructor, and a pilot examiner. He started at Tarom – Romanian Air Transport – in 1994 and has moved up through all the professional ranks: co-pilot on Antonov 24; captain and pilot instructor on ATR 42/72; captain, pilot instructor, and pilot examiner on Airbus A320 and A310; and test pilot and commander of the special flights for the Romanian President and government officials.

In 2001, he became a Type Rating Instructor – codename for instructor of pilots – and since then the pilots he has trained have become captains for at least 12 airlines around the world. He is also a certified Type Rating Examiner by EASA (European Union Aviation Safety Agency), which gives him the authority to decide whether pilots continue to fly or are suspended from flying for a certain period.

He also has vast management experience, having served in different operational and corporate leadership positions inside Tarom, the most important being that of Vice President and Director of Flight Operations.

Emil is an inspiring speaker, invited frequently to address corporate events of different sizes, where he inspires people to higher levels of commitment and professionalism and teaches valuable communication, leadership, and risk management principles.

Emil is a passionate biker, riding with his wife all over Europe on their Harley Davidson as often as they can.

Octavian Pantiș is an entrepreneur. He is the Co-Founder and Managing Partner of Qualians, an international training and consulting company. His firm is dedicated to helping organizations thrive while providing an environment where their people grow professionally, are engaged and have enough time for life outside work. Qualians was named several times "Training Company of the Year" and "Partner Country of the Year" in international networks. He's a partner in two other businesses.

Octavian is also a bestselling author. His two books on productivity and work-life balance, as well as his dozens of articles and hundreds of trainings and speeches on the subject, have brought clarity, motivation, tools and ideas to hundreds of thousands of people from all walks of life. His advice is especially sought after by entrepreneurs and executives at all levels. He was named "Speaker of the Year" and twice "Trainer of the Year" for his inspiring, friendly, and action-oriented style.

His speaking and consultant work includes workshops with senior management teams, as well as speeches for large groups, in person and online, usually on subjects such as leadership, mindset change, and productivity. Octavian is a Professional Member of the USA National Speakers Association.

Octavian spends his time outside work with his wife and three children. Whatever time remains is dedicated to skiing, squash, and studying and collecting old maps.

Find out more about the authors here:
emildobrovolschi.com
octavianpantis.com

Beyond the Book

Inspire your organization and bring this know-how to your team

Captain Emil Dobrovolschi and Octavian Pantiş speak to audiences all over the world in virtual and in-person events, helping individuals, teams and organizations to become better at piloting their responsibilities at work and in life, in these turbulent times.

The know-how you found in this book is also available as training programs, in multiple formats that suit different needs in terms of time, depth, platforms and levels of interaction. Equip your people, especially your leaders, so they are better able to handle and stay on top of the challenges they face.

Drop a quick note at darkcockpitbook.com/contact. We'll respond right away.

Get quantity discounts

The book is available at quantity discounts for orders of 15 or more copies. Orders at darkcockpitbook.com/contact

Visit darkcockpitbook.com for multimedia resources

Go to darkcockpitbook.com for videos from the Full Flight Simulator and even from the cockpit, articles by the authors and video podcasts that go behind the scenes and provide interesting, valuable and actionable insights from the world of aviation. Visit darkcockpitbook.com

Give us your feedback about the book

We would love to hear from you about *Dark Cockpit,* about what you found most valuable in the book, and about how we may be of assistance to you further. Please go to darkcockpitbook.com/feedback

If anyone you know is afraid of flying

Captain Emil Dobrovolschi has made it a personal cause to help people fly with confidence. Get in touch with us if you know people who are afraid of flying because we have prepared a series of resources of different kinds to help them overcome their fear. Please visit darkcockpitbook.com/flyingisgood.

Write a Review

Hey, it's Emil and Octavian here.

We hope you've enjoyed the book, finding it both useful and informative. We have a favor to ask you.

Would you consider giving it a rating wherever you bought the book? Online book stores are more likely to promote a book when they feel good about its content, and reader reviews are a great barometer for a book's quality.

So please go to the website of wherever you bought the book, search for our names and the book title, and leave a review. If able, perhaps consider adding a picture of you holding the book. That increases the likelihood your review will be accepted!

Many thanks in advance,

Capt. Emil Dobrovolschi and Octavian Pantiș

Endnotes

1 www.history.com/on-this-day-in-history/plane-crashes-into-the-Potomac

2 https://corpgov.law.harvard.edu/2018/02/12/ceo-tenure-rates/

3 https://www.britannica.com/topic/US-Airways-Flight-1549-incident

Printed in Great Britain
by Amazon

65792807R00145